COOKING *with the* SAINTS

Cooking

— with the —

SAINTS

*BY ALEXANDRA GREELEY
& FERNANDO FLORES*

SOPHIA INSTITUTE PRESS
Manchester, NH

Cover design by David Ferris Design in collaboration with Perceptions Design Studio.

Interior design by Perceptions Design Studio with contributions from Coronation Media.

Cover photos by Melissa Lew. Cover icon: *Madonna and Child with Saints*, 14th century, by Lippo Memmi (MBECHB) © Peter Horree / Alamy Stock Photo.

Sophia Institute Press
Box 5284, Manchester, NH 03108
1-800-888-9344
www.SophiaInstitute.com

Sophia Institute Press® is a registered trademark of Sophia Institute.

Library of Congress Cataloging-in-Publication Data

Names: Greeley, Alexandra, author.
Title: Cooking with the saints / by Alexandra Greeley and Fernando Flores.
Description: Manchester, New Hampshire : Sophia Institute Press, [2019] | Includes index.

Identifiers: LCCN 2019000236 | ISBN 9781622825103 (hardcover : alk. paper)
Subjects: LCSH: Holiday cooking. | International cooking. | Fasts and feasts—Catholic Church. | Christian saints—Calendar. | Christian saints—Biography.
Classification: LCC TX739 .G74 2019 | DDC 641.5/68—dc23 LC record available at https://lccn.loc.gov/2019000236

TO FATHER EDWARD HATHAWAY,

Rector of the Basilica of St. Mary in Alexandria, Virginia,

whose support of the Cooking with Our Saints

cooking classes inspired this cookbook

Contents

APRIL

MAY

JUNE

JULY

AUGUST

SEPTEMBER

OCTOBER

NOVEMBER

DECEMBER

CELEBRATORY COOKIES

Saints in This Book

Foreword

As the former pastor of St. Veronica Catholic Church in Chantilly, Virginia, I was fortunate to play a small role in the launching and growth of Cooking with Our Saints, a vibrant parish-based apostolate. Since its inception in 2010, Cooking with Our Saints has continued to grow in popularity and has nourished the bodies, souls, and minds of many people of all ages. This book is a beautiful snapshot of the apostolate and a wonderful reference for anyone interested in food, faith, fellowship, and fun.

Through the Incarnation, God came to dwell among us in a particular and profound way in the person of Jesus of Nazareth, who was and is truly God and truly man. Scripture records the exercise of His divinity through miraculous healings, walking on water, the Transfiguration, and ultimately the Resurrection. Scripture also details concrete examples of Jesus' humanity: He was born and grew up in a family; grew tired; wept; experienced hunger and thirst. He experienced firsthand what it is to be human. Over and over again, Jesus acknowledged our human, bodily needs.

> Now the day began to wear away; and the twelve came and said to him, "Send the crowd away, to go into the villages and country round about, to lodge and get provisions; for we are here in a lonely place." But he said to them, "You give them something to eat."
> (Luke 9:12-13)

Cooking with Our Saints is an original, delightful apostolate that echoes that exhortation, "Give them something to eat," while teaching about the lives of many saints. Saints are those heroic men and women who have completed the journey of life on earth, lived it well, and serve as our models and inspiration. The saints and the recipes in this volume call to mind the diverse cultures that were the earthly homes of the saints. They likewise serve as a reminder that, no matter where or when we live, God calls us all to be saints.

This book is a lovely way for everyone to experience the triple nourishment—body, soul, and mind—that Cooking with Our Saints brought to one little Washington metropolitan-area suburb. The recipes here are delicious, authentic, tested, and easily mastered. They come from Alexandra Greeley, a professional chef and author of thirty-five cookbooks! Her partner in many aspects of the apostolate, Fernando Flores, is a tireless world traveler and an advocate of all things relating to food and faith.

I have no doubt that this book will be treasured by many. It is a compilation of delicious recipes, an approachable volume on the lives of saints, and, as the recipes are arranged chronologically according to feast days, it is a wonderful companion to enrich your liturgical year. I expect that this volume will be put to many good uses: by parishes to launch a similar apostolate, by families as a catechetical tool, or by neighbors wanting to start a fun supper club and practice hospitality. I encourage you to dig in, to try out the tasty recipes, and to take time to learn from the rich lives of so many saints.

Very Reverend Edward C. Hathaway

Rector, Basilica of St. Mary

Alexandria, Virginia

Preface

Where would we be without food? Do you realize that food consists not only of nourishment for the body but also of nourishment for the soul? For what other reason would we classify certain foods as "comfort foods"?

This book is a source to satisfy both of these needs. In addition to nutritious meals, it brings nourishment for the soul to the table! Beyond the simple Catholic prayer, "Bless us, O Lord, and these, Thy gifts ..." this book invites you to bring a spiritual dimension to your meals.

By reading about the saints and their commitment to Our Lord, may the cook and any reader experience nourishment of both soul and body as each brings this Catholic heritage to the family table! That's our wish and prayer.

Acknowledgments

Thanking God for the gift of food that sustains life is fundamental. Thanking the saints who have taught us how to serve God recognizes their role in our lives.

And for this book, a special thanks to the priests, St. Veronica parishioners, and many friends who have joined in and helped out with the cooking classes and, ultimately, with assembling this book and testing its recipes. And, of course, we cannot overlook family members who have contributed with their special support of patience and understanding—even recipes.

We are grateful to Sophia Institute Press and its editorial staff for getting it: the book is both a spiritual guide and a how-to on sampling and cooking international recipes. A very special thank-you to agent Robert DiForio, who believed in this project and connected us with the perfect publisher.

Above all, a very special thank-you to Father Edward Hathaway, who opened the door to the series of cooking classes and to this book, which teaches about the divine connection between food and faith in God.

COOKING *with the* SAINTS

Introduction

Most lay Catholics do not realize that the Faith honors more than ten thousand saints. These holy men and women are mentioned in prayers and celebrated on their feast days. The feasts are outlined in the Catholic Church's Tridentine Calendar, a calendar of saints' days throughout the year. Many countries, causes, and entities even have their own patron saints.

Catholic cooks globally have created and dedicated recipes to a variety of popular and even relatively unknown saints. Linking this food-and-faith connection with cooking classes at the Chantilly parish of St. Veronica Catholic Church in Northern Virginia seemed like an appealing idea.

When asked about offering this class at his parish, food-savvy Father Edward Hathaway endorsed the idea. Based on the lives and cuisines of Catholic saints, the classes, called Cooking with Our Saints, became a great success. People from every part of the world live in the Washington, D.C., metro area, so inviting a Catholic speaker from, say, Russia or Syria, was simple. A Cambodian Catholic presented a class about St. John the Apostle Church in her hometown of Siem Riep and taught the students a popular Cambodian dish, Samlar Machuu Pengpa'h Ning Mnoa'h (Pineapple and Tomato Soup).

The classes were always open to all parishioners and, eventually, to others as well. Students paid a minimal fee, learned how to cook an exotic meal, and sat down with pals to eat what they cooked. Often, the priests would stop by and bless the meal beforehand. After eating and cleaning up, the students took home a packet of recipes, a note about the Saint of the Day, and a prayer page with that saint's prayer on it. Students learning to cook foreign fare discovered that food and its special preparation are really gifts from God.

Clearly, then, the underlying incentive for these classes was straightforward: all people should thank God for the gift of food and the gift of life. Without the bounties of nature, no living creature survives. We must embrace and share the love of God with the neediest—those who do not understand or believe in God.

Realizing the universality of this reverence toward saints is inspiring. To that end, this book underscores what the saints teach us: persistence in faith and understanding that God directs us on life's pathways. All people are called to be saints, each in his or her own way. Whether evangelizing, doing works of charity, or quietly living the Faith, all can be an example for others.

Cooking with Our Saints,
St. Veronica Catholic Church (Chantilly, Virginia)

Sacred Days

According to the Roman Rite, the liturgical year begins with Advent, a time of preparation for the celebration of Jesus' birth. The General Roman Calendar lists the celebrations and acknowledgment of feast days and other holy days of the year. For a complete list of these days, visit the website of the United States Conference of Catholic Bishops (USCCB).

HOLY DAYS OF OBLIGATION

In addition to Sundays, in the United States there are six other holy days of obligation on which Catholics must attend Mass.

Solemnity of Mary, the Holy Mother of God (Theotokos), January 1

Catholics honor the Virgin Mother on many feast days in many countries throughout the year. On January 1, however, Catholics celebrate the solemnity of Mary, the Mother of God, Mother of the Church, and our Heavenly Mother. As early as the Council of Ephesus in 431 A.D., Church fathers wanted to honor Mary, and by the seventh century, January 1 was picked as the date to revere the Maternity of the Blessed Virgin Mary. During the following centuries, however, this special feast day was moved to different months, reserving January 1 as the feast of the Circumcision of Christ.

In a 1974 encyclical, Pope Paul VI revised the liturgical year and reassigned January 1 as the solemnity of Mary, the Mother of God. For Christians of the Byzantine Rite and the West, South, and East Syrian Rites, December 26 is their day of Marian celebration.

Ascension Thursday, Forty Days after Easter

In many countries, the Roman Catholic Church has moved this feast day from Thursday to the following Sunday. This feast originated probably as early as the fourth century, and by the fifth century, St. Augustine claimed that the day had apostolic origins. It commemorates Christ's Ascension into heaven.

Solemnity of the Assumption of the Blessed Virgin Mary, August 15

This celebration is the oldest feast day honoring Mary, but the date of its origin is unclear. After the restoration of Jerusalem as a holy city in the year 336 with the building of the Church of the Holy Sepulchre,

memories and records of Mary and the Holy Family reappeared. No record or relics of the burial site of Mary existed. But the apostles found an empty tomb near the site of her death—the Place of Dormition. They decided that her body had risen to heaven. In 1950, Pope Pius XII decreed that the Assumption of Mary is a dogma of the Catholic Church.

Solemnity of All Saints, November 1

Also known as All Saints' Day, this feast began in the early fourth century to honor all those who died as martyrs for Christ. But over the centuries, it has become a day to honor all those who have attained the beatific vision in heaven. These souls are also known as the Church Triumphant. As Catholics commemorate the saints, whether beatified or canonized, they should understand the "universal call to holiness" to join all the saints in heaven. This solemnity is celebrated on November 1.

Solemnity of the Immaculate Conception, December 8

This day became a holy day of obligation in 1854, when Pope Pius IX declared it the day on which Mary was conceived without original sin. This means that she was redeemed from the moment of her conception, full of grace and worthy to be the Mother of the Son of God. She remained pure throughout her life, fulfilling her distinctive role in human history. The Church also proclaims that Mary should be the model for every person's life. Her words to the angel Gabriel, "Let it be done unto me according to thy word," should inspire us all.

Solemnity of the Nativity of Our Lord Jesus Christ, December 25

On this day, Christians celebrate the birth of Jesus Christ. Christmas Day recognizes that "the Word was made flesh"—that is, God's Son came among mankind to show us how to share in His divine life. It is a time for mankind to rejoice and for friends to share "good tidings of great joy that shall be to all the people, for this day is born to you a Savior who is Christ the Lord" (Luke 2:11). According to the revised liturgical calendar, Christmastime begins on the evening of December 24 and ends with the feast of the Baptism of Our Lord.

OTHER HOLY DAYS

Epiphany

This holy day, also known as the feast of the Magi, is traditionally celebrated on January 6, twelve days after Christmas, but in many places has been moved to the Sunday between January 2 and January 8.

The Baptism of the Lord

This day commemorates Jesus' baptism in the Jordan River by John the Baptist. At that time, the Holy Spirit, in the likeness of a dove, descended on Christ when He was in the river.

Candlemas

This holy day, also known as the Presentation of Our Lord and as the Feast of the Purification of the Blessed Virgin, is observed on February 2 in the Latin Rite. It commemorates the day on which Christ was presented in the Temple.

Ash Wednesday

A holy day of fasting and prayer, Ash Wednesday is the first day of Lent, forty days before Easter. Church attendees receive ashen crosses on their foreheads.

Palm Sunday

The Sunday before Easter celebrates Christ's triumphant entry into Jerusalem. Many Christians celebrate this day by carrying palm fronds while marching in a procession. This day marks the beginning of Holy Week.

Holy Thursday

This holy day is the Thursday before Easter. It commemorates the Last Supper that Christ shared with His apostles before His arrest. It also introduces the Holy Eucharist, the gift of Christ's Body and Blood. Many priests honor this day by washing parishioners' feet, as Jesus washed the feet of His apostles.

Good Friday

On this day of fasting and penance, three days before Easter, Christians recall Christ's Passion and death. It is called "good" because Christ saved us from our sins on that day.

Easter Sunday

Also called Resurrection Sunday, this day is a universal celebration of the Resurrection of Christ from the dead. For Christians, it is one of the most important days of the year.

Divine Mercy Sunday

The Sunday after Easter is a celebration of God's mercy. Pope John Paul II established this feast on April 30, 2000, at the canonization of St. Faustina Kowalska.

Pentecost

Pentecost is the seventh Sunday after Easter and marks the day when the Holy Spirit descended on Jesus' disciples after His Ascension.

Solemnity of the Most Holy Trinity

The first Sunday after Pentecost, this day celebrates the three Persons of God: Father, Son, and Holy Spirit.

Solemnity of the Most Holy Body and Blood of Christ

Also known as the solemnity of Corpus Christi, this Sunday celebrates the Real Presence of Christ in the Eucharist. Many churches have Eucharistic processions on this day.

All Souls' Day

Celebrated on November 2 or 3, this day commemorates all the faithful departed. Christians pray for the souls in purgatory, that they may soon enter heaven.

JANUARY

JANUARY 2

ST. BASIL THE GREAT

— Cappadocia, modern-day Turkey —

Born: 330, Died: 379

St. Basil was born to wealthy and devout parents. His siblings include St. Macrina, St. Gregory of Nyssa, St. Naucratius, and St. Peter, bishop of Sebaste.

Studying in Athens, St. Basil befriended St. Gregory of Nazianzen. The two of them would become known as the Cappadocian Fathers, along with St. Gregory of Nyssa. Together, these three men lived an ascetic life in a rustic dwelling, spending their days in prayer and helping the poor.

St. Basil devoted his life to serving God. He was an influential theologian who fought against evil and the heresies of the early Church. Most notably, he became a key advocate of the Nicene Creed.

VASILOPITA
St. Basil's Cake

THIS CAKE TRACES ITS ORIGIN to a centuries-old legend in the tradition of Orthodox Christian families. Throughout his life, St. Basil showed tremendous care for the poor. To help his flock, he negotiated the return of the jewelry and precious coins that the unjust emperor had demanded as a tax from the people. St. Basil baked all of the treasures into one large cake, or "pita," which he distributed among his faithful. Miraculously, each person found his own possessions in the piece of cake he received.

1. Preheat the oven to 350 degrees. Generously grease a 10-inch springform pan. Set aside.

2. Combine the butter and sugar in a large bowl, and using an electric beater on medium speed, mix until they are light and fluffy. Beat in the eggs one at a time until well blended. Fold in the orange and lemon zests.

3. In a separate bowl, sift together 3 cups of the flour, the baking powder, and the salt. Gradually add the milk to the dry mixture, beating after each addition. The batter will be very thick; using a wooden spoon or another sturdy spoon, gradually blend in the remaining flour until the batter is completely smooth.

4. Spread the batter into the pan, press the coin into the batter until it is completely covered (don't let anyone see where you place it!), and then smooth the top. Brush with the egg-and-milk mixture, and sprinkle with sesame seeds. Gently press the blanched almonds into the batter in the form of a cross and, if desired, the current year below it.

5. Bake for 45 minutes or until golden brown. Check after 30 minutes, and loosely cover the cake with foil if you notice that it is browning too quickly. Cool in the pan for 15 minutes. Remove from the pan, and allow the cake to cool thoroughly on a rack before slicing.

INGREDIENTS

SERVES 8 TO 12

1 cup (2 sticks) **unsalted butter**, at room temperature

1 cup **sugar**

3 extra-large **eggs**

Zest of 2 large **oranges**

Zest of 2 large **lemons**

½ teaspoon crushed/powdered **gum mastic** (see note)

4 cups **all-purpose flour**

2 teaspoons **baking powder**

½ teaspoon **salt**

½ cup **whole milk**

1 **egg yolk** blended with 1 tablespoon **whole milk**

Sesame seeds

Blanched almonds

1 **clean coin**, such as a quarter, wrapped in **silver or gold foil**

Gum mastic, or mastic gum, is the dried gum of the mastic tree. It is a traditional seasoning in Greek recipes, but it may be difficult to find. You can omit it from the recipe if it is not readily available.

JANUARY 5

ST. JOHN NEUMANN

— United States —

Born: 1811, Died: 1860

When he came from the Czech Republic to New York in 1836, St. John Neumann was ordained in what is now St. Patrick's Cathedral. He was assigned to work with immigrants near Niagara Falls, where few parish churches existed. Feeling isolated, he applied to the Congregation of the Most Holy Redeemer, commonly known as the Redemptorists, becoming their first "New World" candidate. St. John grew to love the United States and became an American citizen. In 1852, the Holy See appointed him bishop of Philadelphia.

St. John established numerous parish churches, especially within the expanding immigrant communities. He was also the first to institute the diocesan school system, with the opening of several hundred parochial schools.

CHEESECAKE, NEW YORK STYLE

MOST PEOPLE ASSUME THAT ONE OF AMERICA'S MOST POPULAR DESSERTS originated in Philadelphia because the recipe calls for Philadelphia Cream Cheese. Just like St. John Neumann's priesthood, however, Philadelphia Cream Cheese began in New York.

In 1872, a New York dairy farmer developed the enriched creamy cheese product we know today as Philadelphia Cream Cheese. Because Philadelphia was known as the dairy capital in the late nineteenth century, he believed that his creation would enjoy greater popularity if it was marketed as Philadelphia Cream Cheese.

What could be more fitting than this famous dessert to celebrate a saint who started out in New York and became the bishop of Philadelphia? New York and Philadelphia together make most cooks immediately think of cheesecake!

1. Preheat the oven to 325 degrees. Grease or line a 9- or 10-inch deep springform pan with parchment paper, and spray with baking spray. Combine the cookie crumbs with the melted butter, pressing the mixture onto the bottom of the pan.

2. Put the cream cheese into a large mixing bowl. Using an electric mixer on low speed, whip the cream cheese until smooth. Slowly add the sugar to the cream cheese, beating after each addition until the sugar is completely mixed in. Add the eggs, one at a time, again mixing well after each addition. Stir in the cream and vanilla extract, and sprinkle in the cornstarch and salt; mix gently to incorporate fully. Pour the batter into the prepared pan.

3. Bake for 1 to 1½ hours or until the center is firm and a cake tester inserted into the center comes out clean. Remove the outer circle of the pan, and let it cool to room temperature. Cover with foil and refrigerate overnight.

More cream softens the texture of cream cheese and adds moisture.

INGREDIENTS

SERVES 8 TO 10

CRUMB CRUST

2 cups crushed **gingersnaps** or **graham cracker crumbs**

4 tablespoons **butter**, melted

FILLING

3 pounds **Philadelphia cream cheese**, softened

3 cups **sugar**, preferably superfine, or to taste

6 large **eggs**, at room temperature

¼ to ½ cup **heavy cream**, as needed to achieve desired consistency (see note)

3 tablespoons **cornstarch**

2 teaspoons **vanilla extract**

Pinch of **salt**

SAINTLY MEAL *for* JANUARY

ST. ANTHONY THE ABBOT

A Middle Eastern Menu

Fattoush
Cucumber, Tomato, and Feta Cheese Salad

Mahshy Koronb
Egyptian Stuffed Cabbage Rolls

Koshari
Egyptian Rice, Lentils, and Macaroni
with Spicy Tomato Chili Sauce

Kunafa
Shredded Phyllo Cheese Pastry

ST. ANTHONY

— The Abbot —

JANUARY 17

Born:	Died:	
circa 251	circa 356	Patron saint of amputees, animals, and cemetery workers

Born in Egypt, St. Anthony was the son of wealthy, devout Christian parents. When he was twenty years old, he joined a religious group that lived in seclusion, and later he moved to an empty fort in the desert to live alone. He lived there for the next twenty years. In the year 311, St. Anthony traveled to Alexandria to fight Arianism, later returning to a desert cave on Mount Colzim to live again in seclusion. It is believed that he died at the age of 105.

St. Anthony has been credited with inspiring many people to live a holy monastic life; in fact, he founded two monasteries and is considered the founder of Christian monasticism. St. Anthony the Abbot is known by many titles, including Abba Antonius; St. Anthony of Egypt; St. Anthony of the Desert; Patriarch of Monks; St. Anthony the Anchorite; St. Anthony the Great; St. Anthony the Hermit; St. Antonio Abate; Father of Cenobites; and Father of All Monks.

SHOPPING LIST

BAKING SUPPLIES

Semolina, finely ground — 2 tablespoons

Sugar, granulated — 3 cups

BREAD

Pita bread
(or pita chips) — two 4-inch round loaves

CANNED GOODS

Chicken stock
(homemade or canned) — 1 cup

Garbanzo beans, cooked — one 15-ounce can

Tomato sauce — 1¼ cups fresh or canned

Tomato sauce, unseasoned — one 15-ounce can

Vegetable stock — 4 cups

DRY FOODS

Lentils, brown — 1 cup

Macaroni
(small elbow pasta) — 2 cups

Rice, medium-grain — 2 cups

FROZEN FOODS (PASTRIES)

Kunafa dough
(can substitute
shredded phyllo dough) — 1 pound

MEAT

Beef, lean ground — 1 pound

MILK AND DAIRY

Butter, unsalted — 4 tablespoons

Butter, clarified (ghee) — 5 to 6 tablespoons

Feta cheese, sheep's milk,
crumbled — 1 cup

Heavy cream — ½ cup

Mozzarella, finely shredded — 2 cups

Whole milk — 2 cups

OIL AND VINEGAR

Olive oil

Red wine vinegar — 1 tablespoon

Vegetable oil — for deep-frying

PRODUCE

Cabbage, firm white Korean — 3 pounds

Cilantro, fresh — one small bunch

Cucumber, English — 1 large

Dill, fresh — small bunch

Garlic — 2 heads

Lemon — one large

Mint, fresh — one bunch

Onion, red — 1 small

Onion, white — 4 large

Parsley — one small bunch

Tomatoes, Roma — 5

SPICES

Allspice, ground

Baharat spice blend

Bay leaf

Black pepper

Cumin, ground

Red chili flakes

Salt

Sumac, ground

Vanilla extract

Fattoush

Cucumber, Tomato, and Feta Cheese Salad

A classic Middle Eastern and Mediterranean "bread" salad, using stale (here toasted) pita pieces, *fattoush* is a colorful blend of chopped fresh vegetables tossed with a lemony dressing that uses sumac, a popular Middle Eastern spice. The toasted pita pieces add a special crunch to the dish.

Place the cucumber, tomato, red onion, parsley, mint, garlic, lemon juice, sumac, and salt and pepper into a bowl, and stir to combine. Add the pita pieces and feta cheese, and gently toss.

A very popular seasoning in Middle Eastern and Mediterranean countries, the purplish-red spice sumac adds a slightly sour, lemony taste to dishes. As an alternative, you can use lemon zest or a lemon pepper seasoning.

INGREDIENTS

SERVES 4 TO 6

1 large **English cucumber**, diced

3 cups **Roma tomatoes**, chopped

½ **red onion**, peeled and diced

¾ cup **parsley**, chopped

¾ cup **fresh mint**, chopped

1 tablespoon fresh **lemon juice**, or to taste

1½ teaspoons **garlic**, minced, or to taste

1 teaspoon **sumac**, ground (see note)

Salt and freshly ground **black pepper** to taste

Two 4-inch **pita loaves**, toasted and broken into small pieces

1 cup crumbled **sheep's milk feta cheese**, or to taste

Mahshy Koronb

Egyptian Stuffed Cabbage Rolls

Although time consuming to make, these cabbage rolls are a popular Egyptian dish. Preparation time is about 4 hours.

1. Cut away and discard the tough core of the cabbage. Bring to a boil enough water to cover the cabbage. Add the cabbage, and cook about 5 minutes or until the outer leaves are just tender. Remove the outer leaves, and continue to cook the cabbage until the second batch of outer leaves are just tender. Continue cooking until about 25 leaves are loose. Chill the leaves in cold water, and drain well.

2. Heat 2 tablespoons of butter in a saucepan over medium heat, and add the onion. Cook, stirring often, until golden brown. Add ½ cup of tomato sauce, and cook, stirring often, about 5 minutes or until the sauce has thickened. Remove from the heat. Spoon the mixture into a mixing bowl. Add the beef, rice, parsley, mint, dill, cilantro, garlic, black pepper, allspice, and salt. Blend well.

3. Carefully trim away and reserve the tougher center rib of the larger outer cabbage leaves. Cut the largest leaves in half lengthwise. The smaller leaves may remain intact. There should be about 40 or more cabbage pieces.

4. Lay out one leaf at a time on a flat surface. Place 2 teaspoons of the beef mixture in the center of each leaf. Fold the leaf neatly over and around to enclose the filling. Squeeze gently to make the rolls more compact. If desired, slice off the unfilled ends of each roll.

5. Line the bottom of a four-quart saucepan with the leftover cabbage trimmings and leaves. Melt the remaining butter, and pour it over the cabbage trimmings. Add the chicken broth and the remaining tomato sauce. Add the stuffed leaves, and cover them directly with a heat-resistant plate or lid. Put a second lid on the saucepan. Bring to a boil over medium heat, reduce the heat to medium low, and continue to cook for 45 minutes to 1 hour. Check for tenderness, remove from the heat, and serve.

INGREDIENTS

SERVES 4 TO 6

1 or 2 firm white **Napa cabbages**, about 3 pounds

4 tablespoons **unsalted butter**

⅓ cup **onion**, peeled and diced

1 ¼ cups **tomato sauce**, fresh or canned

1 pound lean **ground beef**

⅓ cup **rice** uncooked

2 tablespoons **parsley**, minced

1 teaspoon fresh **mint**, chopped, or to taste

1 teaspoon fresh **dill**, chopped, or to taste

1 teaspoon fresh **cilantro**, minced

1 teaspoon **garlic**, minced

½ teaspoon finely ground **black pepper**

⅛ teaspoon **allspice**, ground

Salt to taste

1 cup **chicken broth**, homemade or canned

Koshari

Egyptian Rice, Lentils, and Macaroni with Spicy Tomato Chili Sauce

The national dish of Egypt, this combination of rice, lentils, and macaroni
has a lengthy history: some sources say home cooks created it in the mid-
nineteenth century. Koshari was enjoyed as an economical dish to use up
extra pantry items. Over the years, the dish has retained its popularity
and is sold out of food carts and in restaurants throughout Egypt.

1. Heat the 2 tablespoons of olive oil in a medium saucepan
   over medium-high heat. Add the rice, and fry it for 2 minutes;
   add the vegetable stock. Bring it to a boil, reduce the heat to
   low, cover, and cook for 15 minutes or until the rice is tender.

2. Rinse the lentils under cold water, and place them in another
   saucepan with 2 cups of water. Add the garlic, cumin, and
   bay leaf, and bring the liquid to a boil. Reduce the heat to
   low, cover, and cook for 20 to 30 minutes or until the lentils
   are tender. Once cooked, add the salt, and stir to combine.
   Strain any excess liquid, if necessary.

3. To make the sauce, heat the oil in a medium saucepan
   over medium heat, and add the onion. Cook until soft and
   translucent, 5 to 7 minutes. Add the garlic, and sauté until
   golden brown. Add the tomato sauce, red wine vinegar,
   baharat, chili flakes (if using), and salt and pepper to taste.
   Cook the mixture over medium heat, reduce the heat to low,
   cover, and cook for 20 minutes, stirring occasionally.

4. To make the crispy onions, heat 2 to 3 tablespoons of oil in a
   skillet. Add the onion slices, and fry until dark brown. Using
   a slotted spoon, remove them from the oil, and place them on
   paper towels to drain and cool.

5. Add the rice, lentils, and cooked macaroni to a large bowl,
   and toss to combine (or simply scoop out desired amounts
   of each onto the plates). Sprinkle a little baharat over each
   portion, and serve topped with some of the tomato sauce.
   Finally, top with garbanzo beans, the crispy onions, and
   another sprinkle of baharat. Serve warm.

INGREDIENTS

SERVES 4

RICE, LENTILS, AND MACARONI

2 tablespoons **olive oil**

1 cup **medium-grain rice**

2 cups **vegetable stock**

1 cup **brown lentils**

1 **garlic clove**, peeled and quartered

1 teaspoon **cumin**, ground

1 **bay leaf**

2 cups **small macaroni**, cooked al dente

½ teaspoon **salt**

SAUCE

2 tablespoons **olive oil**

1 small **onion**, peeled and diced

2 cloves **garlic**, peeled and minced

One 15-ounce can **unseasoned tomato sauce**, puréed

1 tablespoon **red wine vinegar**

2 teaspoons **baharat spice blend** (see note)

¼ teaspoon **red chili flakes** (optional)

Salt and freshly ground **black pepper** to taste

One 15-ounce can **garbanzo beans**, drained and rinsed

GARNISH

2 large **onions**, peeled and thinly sliced

Vegetable oil for frying

*Baharat, which simply means "spice blend," is
a popular Middle Eastern seasoning mixture of
finely ground herbs and spices. It is typically used
to season vegetables, meats, seafood, and soups. It
is common in Middle Eastern markets. You can
make your own spice mixture, or substitute equal
portions of cinnamon, cumin, and paprika.*

Kunafa

Shredded Phyllo Cheese Pastry

Also spelled *kanafeh*, there are several variations of this well-known Arabic dessert. Generally, it consists of a mild white cheese topped with pastry or sandwiched between two pastry layers. Baked or cooked in a thick sugary syrup, it makes a delicious treat.

1. Preheat the oven to 350 degrees. Grease a 10-inch cake pan. Set aside.

2. Melt the clarified butter in a saucepan; set aside. Place the kunafa dough in a big bowl, and using your fingers, separate the sheets. Add the melted butter, and mix thoroughly. Add half of the buttered kunafa dough mix to a cake pan. Press down for a smooth base without lumps.

3. Whisk the milk and semolina together in a saucepan over medium heat until the mixture has thickened. Add the sugar and vanilla, gradually thinning out the mixture with the cream. Using a spatula, cover the entire base of the kunafa dough with the cream mixture, and top with the shredded mozzarella. Top with the remaining kunafa dough mix, again pressing down so that it is completely flat.

4. Bake for 35 minutes or until golden brown. Remove from the oven. Meanwhile, prepare the syrup by cooking the sugar and water in a saucepan over medium heat. Stir occasionally for about 10 minutes. Once the syrup thickens, add the lemon juice, and stir for 2 more minutes. Remove the syrup from the heat, and allow to cool slightly. Pour the syrup over the kunafa evenly, cool for 10 minutes, and serve.

INGREDIENTS

SERVES 4 TO 6

1 pound **kunafa dough** or **shredded phyllo dough**, thawed (see note)

5 to 6 tablespoons **clarified butter (ghee)** (see note)

2 cups **whole milk**

2 tablespoons finely ground **semolina**

4 tablespoons **sugar**

1 tablespoon **vanilla extract**

½ cup **heavy cream**

2 cups finely shredded **mozzarella**

SYRUP

2 cups **sugar**

1 cup **water**

Juice from ½ small **lemon**

Look for shredded phyllo pastry in the freezer of your local supermarket, or visit a Middle Eastern market and buy kunafa dough.

You can make your own clarified butter, also known as ghee, or simply purchase it from an Indian or Asian market.

Quote from
ST. ANTHONY THE ABBOT

"The devil is afraid of us when we pray and make sacrifices. He is also afraid when we are humble and good. He is especially afraid when we love Jesus very much. He runs away when we make the Sign of the Cross."

JANUARY 24

ST. FRANCIS DE SALES

— France —

Born: 1567, Died: 1622

St. Francis de Sales was born into a noble family in the Kingdom of Savoy, near Geneva, Switzerland. He received a privileged education at prominent schools, and, by historical accounts, he led a life of gentlemanly decorum among the nobility.

As a priest, St. Francis became an avid evangelist in an area filled with staunch Calvinists; several times he escaped murder. In 1602, the bishop of Geneva died, and St. Francis was appointed his successor. During his years as bishop of Geneva, he attained a reputation as a great homilist. His writings, especially his *Introduction to the Devout Life*, and his many efforts on behalf of the Church contribute to his legacy.

DUCK BREAST
WITH PORT WINE SAUCE

THE FRENCH HAVE DEVOTED MUCH TIME AND ENERGY to perfecting the duck breast, or *magret de canard*. Recipes include duck meat in casseroles, and braised, roasted, and seared duck. As usual, most recipes include some wine and fruit or vegetables, such as this version. Serve the breasts with a side of mashed potatoes and steamed green beans.

1. Pat the duck breasts dry with a paper towel, and score the skin side with a small sharp knife in a lattice pattern. Sprinkle with the salt, and season generously with the pepper.

2. Pour the olive oil into a nonstick skillet, and heat over medium heat. Place the breasts in it, skin side down. Cook for 10 minutes or until crisp and golden. Turn and cook for another 10 minutes. Remove the breasts from the skillet, leaving about 1 tablespoon of liquid in the pan. Keep the breasts warm.

3. Add the shallots, onion, and sugar to the skillet, and cook over medium heat until softened and lightly caramelized, about 5 minutes. Add the vinegar, increase the heat to medium high, and cook until the liquid has evaporated. Stir in the port and any juices that have come from the duck breasts. Cook over medium-high heat for 2 to 3 minutes until slightly reduced. Remove from the heat, and stir in the butter.

4. Cut each breast lengthwise into ¼-inch-thick slices, and fan four or five slices on a dinner plate. Spoon a tablespoon of sauce over the duck, and serve at once with a selection of vegetables.

INGREDIENTS

SERVES 4

4 **duck breast fillets**, about 8 ounces each, skin on

2 teaspoons **sea salt**

1 teaspoon freshly ground **black pepper**

2 tablespoons **olive oil**

2 **shallots**, peeled and finely chopped

1 cup **onion**, finely chopped

1 tablespoon **sugar**

1 tablespoon **wine vinegar**

½ cup **ruby port** or **Madeira**

3 tablespoons **unsalted butter**

Each Musgovy duck breast lobe (half a duck's breast fillet) weighs at least 8 ounces and up to 18 ounces. Adjust size to appetites. You can substitute Pekin or Moulard duck breast, which weigh about a pound each, bringing the fillet weight to 8 ounces.

JANUARY 28

ST. THOMAS AQUINAS
—Italy—

Born: circa 1225, Died: 1274

St. Thomas Aquinas had a brilliant, perceptive mind. At the age of five, he became a student at the Benedictine Abbey of Monte Cassino. Later, he moved on to the University of Naples and studied the classical philosophers, such as Aristotle, Plato, and Socrates.

St. Thomas was so attracted to the holy life that at the age of nineteen he entered the newly formed Order of St. Dominic, becoming the community's most notable member. His best-known work, which remains unfinished, is the *Summa Theologica*, a five-volume summary of the relationship between God and man. It is an instructional manual for theology students, seminarians, and laity that summarizes all the main teachings of the Catholic Church.

STAR-SHAPED COOKIES

MAKES ABOUT 3 DOZEN 5-INCH COOKIES

THE STAR IS A SYMBOL OF THE BRIGHT LIGHT OF INTELLECT and, therefore, an appropriate shape to associate with St. Thomas Aquinas. If you wish, you can decorate or ice the cookies once they are completely cool. This recipe works well with other cookie cutters, should you choose another specially themed shape. The recipe creator has called it officially "The Holy Name of Mary" cookie.

1. Preheat the oven to 400 degrees. Line baking sheets with parchment paper, and set aside.

2. Sift together the flour, baking powder, and salt, and set aside. In a separate bowl, using an electric mixer on medium speed, whip together the butter and sugar until smooth and creamy. Stir in the eggs, vanilla, and lemon extract. Reduce the speed to low, gradually add the flour mixture, and beat until well combined. Add the milk, and continue beating until the dough clumps together.

3. Divide the dough in half. Generously sprinkle a work surface with flour. Roll the dough out to ¼-inch thickness. Using a star-shaped cookie cutter, cut out the shapes, and place them on a baking sheet, leaving space between each cookie. Repeat until the dough is used up.

4. Bake for 10 to 12 minutes or until the edges turn golden. Remove from the oven, and cool on wire racks.

INGREDIENTS

3 ½ cups **all-purpose flour**, or more as needed

2 teaspoons **baking powder**

1 teaspoon **salt**

1 cup (2 sticks) **unsalted butter**, at room temperature

1 cup **sugar**

2 large **eggs**, lightly beaten

1 teaspoon **vanilla extract**

1 teaspoon **lemon extract**, or more to taste

¼ cup **whole milk**

FEBRUARY

FEBRUARY 1

ST. BRIGID OF KILDARE
— Ireland —

Born: circa 451, Died: circa 521

St. Brigid of Kildare was a high-spirited youngster with a kindly heart. Perhaps listening to St. Patrick as a child made an indelible impression on her. She could not bear to see others cold or hungry, and she often gave away her father's possessions.

St. Brigid refused to marry. She instead went to her bishop and took her first vows. With the other Sisters of her community, she later founded a convent called Kildare Abbey, which became a center of religious learning.

As an abbess, St. Brigid established many convents throughout Ireland. She also gained a reputation for her ability to heal. Even bishops sought her advice. She became known as the "Mary of the Gaels."

ST. BRIGID'S OATCAKES

THESE CHEWY CAKES have been popular with Irish children for years. Resembling scones, these are healthful, and parents can boost flavor and appeal with butter and jam. The oatcakes are probably similar to what St. Brigid enjoyed at mealtimes. They are also known as "Irish Oatcakes."

1. One day ahead, combine the oats and buttermilk in a small bowl. Blend thoroughly, cover, and refrigerate overnight.

2. When ready to cook, preheat the oven to 350 degrees. Line a baking sheet with parchment paper, and set aside.

3. Remove the oat mixture from the refrigerator. Combine the flour, dried fruit, baking soda, salt, cinnamon, baking powder, and allspice in a large bowl. Cut in the butter and brown sugar with a pastry blender until the butter is the size of peas. Mix in the soaked oats, and knead the dough until it comes together and is smooth. The dough should be fairly dry, but if necessary, add a few drops of water to help bring it together. Form the dough into a round shape about 1 inch thick. Place the round on the prepared baking sheet. Cut the round into 6 wedges, and separate the wedges slightly.

4. Bake for 25 to 30 minutes or until a slight crust forms and a cake tester inserted into the thickest part comes out clean. Let cool.

INGREDIENTS

SERVES 6 OR MORE

2 cups uncooked **old-fashioned rolled oats**

1 ¼ cups **buttermilk**

2 ½ cups sifted **all-purpose flour**

½ cup dried fruit, such as **raisins** or **coarsely chopped apricots**

1 teaspoon **baking soda**

1 teaspoon **salt**

1 teaspoon **cinnamon**, ground

½ teaspoon **baking powder**

¼ teaspoon **allspice**, ground

¼ cup **unsalted butter**, softened

¼ cup **brown sugar**

Vegetable oil spray

FEBRUARY 2

The Presentation of Our Lord

*The Feast of the Purification
of the Blessed Virgin Mary*

Candlemas

OUR LADY OF
COPACABANA

— *Bolivia* —

Francisco Yupanqui, who wanted
his hometown of Copacabana to be
dedicated to Our Lady, toiled to learn
the basics of carving so that he could
chisel a wooden statue of the Virgin and
Child. After months of fervent work,
Francisco completed what is known as
Our Lady of Copacabana. When he
presented his statue to the town, all were
stunned by the beauty and grace of his
carvings.

Numerous miracles have been attributed
to Our Lady. A church was built to
house her statue, and pilgrims came
daily to shower her with jewels and
other finery. Each February, people still
travel from afar to honor the Patroness
of Bolivia.

SILPANCHO

SERVES 8

Silpancho, derived from the Quechua word *Sillip'anchu*, is the name of a popular Bolivian dish from the city of Cochabamba. A substantial offering featuring rice, potatoes, a salad, slices of sizzled beef, and fried eggs, all carefully layered for a tempting dish, silpancho is really a meal in itself.

Bolivians have created variations of the traditional dish by dicing the meat and cooking it with the rice or using different seasoning ingredients such as soy sauce. It's worth noting that Bolivians love this dish so much that they may eat it for breakfast, lunch, or dinner. They even make a sandwich of it called *trancapecho*, which contains all the ingredients of silpancho. The onion and tomato salad can be offered separately if someone doesn't eat spicy foods. The *locoto* pepper (also known as *rocoto* in Peru) may be available online, but the jalapeño is a fine substitute.

POTATOES

Once potatoes are almost fully cooked in boiling water, 18 to 20 minutes, peel off the skin and let them cool. When cool, slice them into thick pieces. Heat the oil in a skillet over medium heat, and fry the slices on both sides until golden.

POTATOES INGREDIENTS

8 medium **red-skin potatoes**, boiled, peeled, and cut into thick slices

3 tablespoons **vegetable oil** for frying, or more as needed

RICE

Heat about 2 tablespoons of oil in a pot over medium-high heat, and add the rice. Fry the rice until most of the grains have changed color. Reduce the heat to low, and add the boiling water and salt; sprinkle in garlic powder or add some crushed garlic, and add some minced onions. Cover, and cook for 12 minutes. Turn the heat off without removing the pot from the heat. It will finish cooking in a few minutes.

RICE INGREDIENTS

2 cups uncooked **white rice**

2 tablespoons **vegetable oil** for frying, or more as needed

3 ½ cups boiling **water**

1 to 2 teaspoons **salt** (optional)

Garlic powder or crushed **garlic** to taste

Minced **onions**, dry or raw, to taste

SALAD

Cut all the ingredients as indicated, put into a large bowl, and mix with the vinegar, oil, and salt.

SALAD INGREDIENTS

1 large **white onion**, peeled and thinly sliced

2 medium **tomatoes**, cubed

Apple cider vinegar to taste

2 to 3 tablespoons **canola** or other **vegetable oil**

2 tablespoons fresh **parsley**, chopped

1 **locoto** or **jalapeño pepper**, thinly sliced (optional)

Salt to taste

MEAT

To prepare the meat, sprinkle each slice with salt and pepper. Using a meat pounder, pound each slice until very thin and large, about the size of a dinner plate. Sprinkle a generous amount of bread crumbs on the meat, and pound the meat again so that the crumbs stick to it; repeat on the other side. Heat a nonstick skillet over medium heat, and add a few tablespoons of oil. Fry the meat on both sides until it is cooked. Turn each slice carefully so the bread crumbs stick and don't burn. When the meat is cooked, set aside. Fry the eggs, preferably over medium; add more oil, if needed.

MEAT INGREDIENTS

About 2 pounds **beef tenderloin** or **round steak** (use a very thin cut), cut into 8 uniform slices

Salt and freshly ground **black pepper** to taste

2 cups regular **bread crumbs**

2 tablespoons **vegetable oil**, or more as needed

8 large **eggs**

ASSEMBLE THE DISH

To serve, spoon ½ cup rice onto a dinner plate, and add a large spoonful of potato wedges. Top the rice and potatoes with a slice of fried meat, and finish with one over-medium egg. Garnish this with the salad, and serve.

SAINTLY
MEAL
for
FEBRUARY

❧

ST. PAUL MIKI

A Simple Japanese Meal

Oyako Donburi
Chicken and Egg Rice Bowl

Misoshiru
Miso Soup

Inarizushi
Fried Tofu Pockets

ST. PAUL MIKI

FEBRUARY 6

Born:	Died:	
circa 1562	1597	Patron saint of Japan

St. Paul Miki was born in the city of Tounucumada, Japan. At a young age, he joined the Society of Jesus, working alongside several European missionaries. They taught the Gospel in the city of Nagasaki, building upon the earlier missionary work of St. Francis Xavier. As Catholicism spread rapidly, influential Buddhists and other leaders felt threatened by the growth of the Faith.

When the emperor Hideyoshi ordered Catholicism to be banished from the country, Jesuits were forced to go underground to operate. In the next decade, direct persecution broke out, possibly prompted by the gossip of a boasting Spanish merchant. He convinced the emperor that St. Paul Miki and his fellow missionaries were conspiring to help a European invasion of Japan. The fearful emperor ordered twenty-six missionaries and laypeople, including Jesuits and Franciscans, adults and youths, to be arrested and killed. The martyrs were forced to walk six hundred miles through snow from Kyoto to Nagasaki. On February 5, 1597, they were tied with ropes and chains to crosses while executioners stood by with swords. Accounts of the scene report that all twenty-six young men fixed their eyes on St. Paul and sang the Canticle of Zechariah. The martyrs were canonized in 1862 by Pope Pius IX.

SHOPPING LIST

BAKING SUPPLIES

Sugar, granulated   3 tablespoons

CANNED GOODS

Japanese stock (Dashi)
or chicken broth   4 cups

CONDIMENTS

Miso paste, red or white   3 to 4 tablespoons

Soy sauce   6 tablespoons

DAIRY

Eggs, large   4 or 5

Silken tofu   one 8-ounce block

DRY GOODS

Japanese rice, cooked   6 to 8 cups

PRODUCE

Onions   2 medium

Scallions   5

MEAT

Chicken, boneless   ¼ pound

MISCELLANEOUS

Japanese rice wine (sake) 1 cup

Fried tofu pockets
(inarizushi), prepared   as many as desired

Oyako Donburi

Chicken and Egg Rice Bowl

The Japanese name *oyako donburi* translates as "parent-and-child donburi"—an indication that both chicken and an egg (parent and child) are basic ingredients of this dish. Note that a donburi is a Japanese rice bowl topped with cooked ingredients, usually chicken, but some versions use beef instead. Be sure to use the short-grain Japanese rice sold at Asian markets; long-grain rice doesn't stick together after cooking and therefore will not work in this recipe. You will get the best meat flavor starting with raw chicken, but you may also use leftover chicken. With this meal-in-a-bowl serve hot green tea and a starter of a clear soup, such as miso soup.

1. Set the cooked rice aside, keeping it covered and warm. Mix the eggs gently with chopsticks or a fork, and set aside. Assemble the chicken, cut-up onions, and sliced scallions, and set aside.

2. Combine the sauce ingredients in a saucepan, and cook over medium heat. Add the chicken, and cook uncovered for 5 to 8 minutes. Add the onion, and cook 1 minute more; adjust the seasonings as needed.

3. Stir the eggs again, and pour them gently in a steady stream around the chicken in the simmering sauce. Let the eggs spread naturally, and do not stir. Once they start to bubble at the edges, stir the eggs once. After 1 minute, remove from the heat, and leave for a moment to finish cooking.

4. To serve, scoop 1½ to 2 cups of hot rice into a donburi or a deep soup bowl. Using a large spoon, scoop some of the chicken and egg topping and the sauce over the rice. The sauce will seep down into the rice, but the rice will not be soupy. Garnish with a sprinkling of sliced scallions, and serve.

INGREDIENTS

SERVES 4 TO 6

RICE BOWL

6 to 8 cups hot cooked **Japanese rice**

4 or 5 large **eggs**

¼ pound **boneless chicken**, diced

2 medium **onions**, peeled and sliced or diced

2 to 4 **scallions**, including the green stems, thinly sliced

SAUCE

1 cup **sake** (Japanese rice wine)

1 cup **dashi** (Japanese stock) or **chicken broth**

6 tablespoon **soy sauce**

3 tablespoons **sugar**

Misoshiru

Miso Soup

INGREDIENTS

SERVES 4 TO 6

3 cups **dashi** (Japanese stock) or **chicken broth**

One 8-ounce block **silken tofu**, diced

3 to 4 tablespoons **red** or **white miso paste**

¼ cup **scallions**, chopped

The Japanese seasoning miso is made by fermenting rice, barley, or soybeans with salt and the fungus known as *kōji-kin*. The resulting thick paste is used in numerous ways, from making sauces to pickling meats and vegetables, and for mixing with dashi soup stock to make *misoshiru*, or miso soup. This protein- and vitamin-rich paste has been a Japanese culinary staple since feudal times, and its popularity has spread universally so that Asian and some well-stocked Western markets carry it. The white miso paste has a sweet taste and is best used for a light soup or sauce. The red miso paste has fermented longer and has a deep savory flavor that can overwhelm mild dishes but is perfect for hearty soups, sauces, and glazes. Dashi soup stock is a basic ingredient in many Japanese dishes, especially soups and stews. Like miso paste, dashi stock, either as a paste, granules, or dried, is sold in Asian markets and in many Western markets.

1. In a saucepan, bring the dashi soup stock to a boil over medium heat. Spoon out some of the hot stock from the saucepan, and dissolve the miso in it, stirring well. Pour the miso mixture back into the soup, and stir gently. Continue to cook over low heat for 1 to 2 minutes, and stir in the diced tofu. Cook for 3 to 4 more minutes, and add the chopped scallions.

2. Serve hot.

Inarizushi

Fried Tofu Pockets

A unique Japanese treat, inarizushi is a small pocket or pouch of deep-fried tofu that contains either cooked sushi rice, cooked vegetables, or other ingredients. Since these are difficult to make at home, Japanese cooks purchase their inarizushi from markets and stuff them with their choice of savory or sweet fillings. Serve immediately.

Final Words of

ST. PAUL MIKI

"The only reason for my being killed is that
I have taught the doctrine of Christ. I thank
God it is for this reason that I die. I believe that
I am telling the truth before I die. I know you
believe me, and I want to say to you all once
again: Ask Christ to help you become happy. I
obey Christ. After Christ's example, I forgive
my persecutors. I do not hate them. I ask God
to have pity on all, and I hope my blood will
fall on my fellow men as a fruitful rain."

FEBRUARY 15

ST. CLAUDE DE LA COLOMBIÈRE

— France —

Born: 1641, Died: 1682

As rector of the Jesuit community at Paray-le-Monial, St. Claude de la Colombière became spiritual director to Sister Margaret Mary Alocoque. She described private revelations from Christ, asking her to promote devotion to His Sacred Heart. St. Claude was convinced of the validity of her visions and zealously promoted the devotion himself.

He was later appointed to the Court of the Duchess of York. Despite hostility toward Catholics in England at that time, St. Claude continued to preach and lead to reconciliation those who had abandoned the Faith.

Eventually, St. Claude was falsely accused of involvement in a papist plot and imprisoned. The appalling conditions had ruined his health by the time he was finally extradited to France.

TARTE NORMANDE
Normandy Apple Tart

THE AMOUNT OF ALMOND CREAM may seem small, but it expands as it bakes and surrounds the fruit slices. Be sure to work quickly when rolling out the Sweet Pastry Shell dough, but don't worry if it tears—it can easily be patched with a small piece of dough. If you are substituting a frozen pie shell, use a 9- or 10-inch shallow pie shell, not one designed for a deep-dish pie. The following recipe is separated into two parts: the pastry shell and the almond cream.

1. In a food processor, grind the almonds with 2 tablespoons of sugar to a fine powder. Set mixture aside.

2. Prepare or purchase the sweet pastry shell, and prepare the almond cream according to the directions on the next page.

3. Spread the almond cream evenly over the bottom of the sweet pastry shell. Cut the apple halves into thin crosswise slices, keeping each half together. Using a metal spatula, set the apple halves on the almond cream at equal distances, with slices radiating outward from the center like spokes. Press slightly to flatten the slices.

4. Preheat the oven to 425 degrees.

5. Place the tart on a heated baking sheet in the lower third of the oven. Bake for 10 minutes. Reduce the temperature to 350 degrees, and bake until the almond cream is set and golden brown, about 30 minutes more. Remove from the oven, and cool on a wire rack.

6. Heat the preserves with rum, kirsch, or vanilla over low heat, stirring often until melted. Strain mixture. Brush over the top of the tart. Serve at room temperature.

INGREDIENTS

SERVES 8

SWEET PASTRY SHELL (see the ingredients on the next page) or one **9- or 10-inch unbaked pie shell**

ALMOND CREAM (see the recipe on the next page)

3 medium **Golden Delicious apples**, peeled, halved, and cored

⅓ cup **apricot preserves**

1 tablespoon **rum** or **kirsch** or 1 teaspoon **vanilla extract**

SWEET PASTRY SHELL

7. Combine the flour, sugar, and salt in a food processor and process for 2 or 3 seconds. Scatter the butter pieces over the flour mixture. Pulse until the mixture resembles coarse meal. Add the egg, and pulse again, scraping down occasionally, until the dough forms sticky crumbs that can easily be pressed together. If the dough is dry, add ½ teaspoon of cold water and process again. Transfer the dough to a work surface.

8. Blend the dough by pushing a quarter of it away from you and spreading it with the heel of your hand against the work surface. Repeat with the remaining dough in 3 batches. Shape the dough into a flat disk. Wrap it in plastic wrap, and refrigerate it for 4 hours or up to 2 days.

9. Lightly butter a 9- or 10-inch round metal tart pan with removable base. Remove the dough from the refrigerator, and let it soften for 1 minute. Lightly flour a cold surface, and roll the dough out into a ¼-inch-thick round shape, at least 1 inch larger than your pan size across. Wrap it loosely around a floured rolling pin, and unroll the dough over the pan. Ease the dough into the pan.

10. Using your thumb, push the dough down slightly at the top edge of the pan. Roll the rolling pin across the pan to cut off the dough. With your finger and thumb, push up the top edge of the dough so it is ¼ inch higher than the rim of the pan. Pierce the dough all over with a fork. Cover, and refrigerate 1 hour or overnight.

ALMOND CREAM

Cream the butter and the ½ cup sugar with an electric mixer until light and fluffy. Add the remaining 6 tablespoons sugar, and beat until mixture is smooth. Gradually beat in the egg and egg yolk. Stir in the almonds, rum or vanilla, and flour.

SWEET PASTRY SHELL INGREDIENTS

1 ½ cups **all-purpose flour**

6 tablespoons **sugar**

¼ teaspoon **salt**

½ cup **unsalted butter**, very cold, cut into bits

1 large **egg**, lightly beaten

ALMOND CREAM INGREDIENTS

6 tablespoons **unsalted butter**

½ cup plus 6 tablespoons **sugar**

1 large **egg**

1 **egg yolk**

⅔ cup **blanched almonds**, whole or slivered

2 teaspoons **rum** or **kirsch** or 1 teaspoon **vanilla**

2 tablespoons unbleached **all-purpose flour**

FEBRUARY 20

STS. FRANCISCO AND JACINTA MARTO

— Portugal —

Born: 1908, Francisco; 1910, Jacinta
Died: 1919, Francisco; 1920, Jacinta

Our Lady of the Rosary first appeared near Fátima, Portugal, to brother and sister Francisco and Jacinta Marto and their cousin, Lucia de Jesus Santos. She asked the children to pray the Rosary for world peace, the end of World War I, and the conversion of communist Russia. At each subsequent apparition, growing numbers of people were present.

On October 13, after heavy rains, about seventy thousand people gathered. When Mary appeared and opened her hands, the clouds dispersed, and the sun began to spin earthward, its heat drying the ground.

Francisco and Jacinta both died of influenza as children. Lucia survived, becoming a Carmelite nun. She was still alive when Francisco and Jacinta were beatified in 2000.

CALDO VERDE
Green Vegetable Soup

A TRADITIONAL DISH THAT ORIGINATED in northern Portugal in the Minho Province (now known as Entre-Douro-e-Minho), this soup includes greens such as cabbage, kale, spinach, or collards; potatoes; and sometimes onions and garlic. Some cooks include sausage, such as the Portuguese chorizo or linguiça, and serve this hearty dish with bread, often Portuguese cornbread. A national favorite not only in Portugal but wherever Portuguese immigrants live, such as Macau, it is often served for both celebratory and everyday meals.

1. Combine the potatoes and onions with 2 quarts of water in a large saucepan. Bring the water to a boil over medium heat, and cook the vegetables until tender, about 20 minutes. Add the olive oil and the salt and pepper.

2. Add the chopped spinach and kale along with the slices of sausage, and cook for about 5 minutes or until the greens have wilted. Adjust the seasonings. Serve the soup immediately.

INGREDIENTS
SERVES 4 TO 6

4 whole **potatoes**, peeled and cubed

2 **large onions**, peeled and cubed

2 tablespoons **olive oil**

Salt and freshly ground **black pepper** to taste

½ pound **spinach**, rinsed, trimmed, and chopped

½ pound **kale**, rinsed, trimmed, and chopped

1 pound **Portuguese-style sausage**, cooked and sliced

MARCH

MARCH 3

ST. KATHARINE DREXEL

— United States —

Born: 1858, Died: 1955

As a young woman, St. Katharine Mary Drexel received an excellent education and led a privileged life. Things changed dramatically, however, when she nursed her stepmother through a terminal illness. St. Katharine realized that regardless of family fortune, no amount of money could prevent suffering. At age thirty-one, she joined the Sisters of Mercy convent in Pittsburgh.

With several other nuns, St. Katharine founded the Sisters of the Blessed Sacrament to aid Native Americans and African Americans. Her congregation opened its first mission boarding school in Santa Fe, New Mexico. Other schools soon followed. By the mid-1900s, the number of religious institutions that St. Katharine's order had founded numbered 145 missions, 49 elementary schools, and 12 high schools.

PHILADELPHIA CHEESESTEAK SANDWICH

SERVED ON A LONG, SOFT ROLL, the typical cheesesteak sandwich features thinly sliced, griddled ribeye or round steak and American cheese, Cheez Whiz, or provolone topped with sautéed onions and bell peppers, spiked with mustard and hot sauce. Variations exist using chicken, lettuce, and tomatoes, and even a vegan version.

The following recipe was devised by a since-deceased Philadelphia native who claimed that this mirrored the original cheesesteak sandwich he enjoyed as a child. As Mr. Leonetti once posted, "The old authentic way uses Provolone Cheese … deli roast beef … top round sliced wafer thin or frozen Rib-Eye roast shaved on an electric slicer.… If you make any changes with the ingredients or the directions, it will not be the same."

1. Hollow out some of the soft white bread from the inside of each half, and set aside.

2. Heat a griddle or a large skillet over medium-high heat. When hot, cover the bottom with olive oil. Add the onion and bell pepper, and cook, stirring, until caramelized, 6 to 8 minutes. Add the garlic, salt, and pepper, and cook for about 30 seconds. Push the mixture to one side of the griddle, or remove it from the skillet.

3. Place the meat on the hot part of the griddle or in the skillet. Using 2 spatulas while cooking, cut the meat into smaller pieces. Cook for about 2 minutes or until the meat is no longer pink. Mix the meat with the caramelized onions and bell pepper. Divide the mixture into 2 portions, and top each with the cheese to melt.

4. When the cheese is melted, and with 1 or 2 spatulas, layer the meat, cheese, and cooked vegetables on the bottom half of each roll. Add the marinara sauce, as desired. Place the top half over the filling, and serve immediately.

INGREDIENTS

SERVES 2

Extra virgin olive oil for cooking

½ **white onion**, peeled and thinly sliced

½ **green bell pepper**, seeded and thinly sliced

2 teaspoons **garlic**, minced

Salt and freshly ground **black pepper** to taste

1 loaf **Italian bread**, or 1 loaf **French bread**, or 2 large **hoagie** or **sub rolls**

½ pound **deli roast beef**, very rare, sliced wafer thin

½ pound **provolone cheese**, thinly sliced

Marinara sauce, as needed

MARCH 10

ST. JOHN OGILVIE

— Scotland —

Born: 1579, Died: 1615

St. John Ogilvie came from a noble Scottish family with a staunch Calvinist father. Catholicism having all but disappeared from Scotland, St. John knew nothing about the Faith until he studied in continental Europe.

He converted to Catholicism at age seventeen, soon becoming a Jesuit priest. He requested to be sent back to Glasgow to serve Scotland's few Catholics. By that time, the Catholic Faith had become illegal in Scotland.

Disguised as a horse trader, St. John returned to Scotland, preaching and celebrating Mass. When he was captured and arrested, he refused to renounce his Faith and was imprisoned, tortured, and condemned to death. In 1615, at age thirty-six, he was hanged and drawn on the Glasgow Cross.

CLAPSHOT

THIS IS A TYPICAL SCOTTISH VEGETABLE DISH, made with potatoes and turnips. It is served with oatcakes, haggis, or another type of meat entrée. The dish originated in Orkney or Northern Scotland and was traditionally made with bacon fat, not butter. The best version calls for very starchy potatoes; in Scotland, the traditional name for a potato is "tattie."

Cook the potatoes and the turnips separately in boiling water until fork tender, about 20 minutes each. Meanwhile, heat 2 tablespoons of butter over medium heat, and cook the onion, stirring until soft but not browned, about 5 to 6 minutes. When the potatoes and turnips are tender, drain and combine them in a large bowl. Using a fork or potato masher, mash the two together with the remaining butter and the sautéed onions. Once well combined, stir in the chives and seasoning to taste. Serve hot.

INGREDIENTS

SERVES 4

1 pound starchy **potatoes**, peeled and chopped

1 pound **turnips**, peeled and chopped

3 tablespoons **unsalted butter** or **bacon fat**

1 **onion**, peeled and diced

2 tablespoons **chives**, chopped

Salt and freshly ground **black pepper** to taste

MARCH 17

ST. PATRICK

— *Ireland* —

Born: circa 385, Died: circa 461

Although born in England, St. Patrick is known as the "Apostle of Ireland." On his feast day, millions of people hold parades, wear green, and drink pints of Irish stout. But these celebrations have little to do with the real St. Patrick.

Who was the real St. Patrick? At age sixteen, bandits captured St. Patrick and sold him to an Irish chieftain. As a slave, he tended his master's sheep for years, praying frequently. At the urging of an angel, he escaped back to Britain and became a priest.

After receiving an angelic message to return to pagan Ireland as a missionary, St. Patrick began his work: he baptized many thousands, ordained priests, and founded convents for women.

COTTAGE PIE

A COMFORTING MEAL TO WARD OFF WINTER CHILLS, this Irish dish is composed of ground beef (a shepherd's pie is made with minced lamb; often people confuse the two dishes) and is topped with mashed potatoes. In the past, cooks made this dish to use up leftover meats and lined the baking dish with mashed potatoes as well as using them as a topping. Depending on the cook's on-hand supplies, the pie may contain vegetables, such as peas, chopped carrots, and diced celery. The dish is usually moistened with a hearty gravy. Some historians say that cooks created the dish in Scotland and Northern England.

Chef Terry Walline says about the roux, or thickener: "Using oil or butter is just a flavor preference depending upon what you are thickening. A quick reheat and stir will loosen it so it will pour out of the pan slowly while thickening your liquid. The key is to drizzle in the roux while whisking so you don't over-thicken your liquid. Liquid must be at least 185 degrees for it to thicken; this also applies to whitewashes using arrowroot or corn starch as a thickening agent, in case you want to make this recipe gluten-free."

The following recipe is separated into three parts: first the mashed potato topping, then the roux, and finally the meat filling.

MASHED POTATO TOPPING

1. Place the potatoes in a medium saucepan, and cover them with cold water. Cover, and bring to a boil over high heat. Once boiling, uncover, reduce the heat to medium low, and cook until fork tender, about 20 minutes. Drain the potatoes, and return them to the saucepan. Mash the potatoes while adding butter, milk, and salt and pepper, and continue to mash until smooth. Set aside.

2. Preheat the oven to 400 degrees.

TOPPING INGREDIENTS

1 ½ pounds **potatoes**, peeled and cubed

3 to 4 tablespoons **unsalted butter**

Milk, as needed

Salt and freshly ground **black pepper** to taste

¼ pound **sharp Irish cheddar**, shredded

1 cup **scallions**, diced

THE ROUX

To make the roux, melt the butter over medium heat, and whisk in the flour. Cook until the flour is absorbed, 2 to 3 minutes. Turn off the heat. (For more thickener, repeat this step with more ingredients.)

ROUX INGREDIENTS

1 cup **unsalted butter**

1 cup **all-purpose flour**

THE MEAT FILLING

1. Place 1 tablespoon of vegetable oil in a 12-inch sauté pan, and heat over medium-high heat. Add the ground beef, and cook until browned and cooked throughout, 6 to 8 minutes; drain off the fat. Add the onions, peas, carrots, and garlic, and sauté until they begin to turn golden, 5 to 6 minutes. Add the beer, wine, beef broth, basil, oregano, and sage, and stir to combine. Bring to a rapid boil, and whisk in the roux slowly to thicken to the desired consistency; reduce the heat to low; add salt and pepper to taste, and cook 1 to 2 minutes.

2. Spread the meat filling evenly in a 9 x 9-inch baking dish. Top with the mashed potato topping, starting around the edges to create a seal to prevent the mixture from bubbling up, and smooth with a spatula. Place on the middle rack of the oven.

3. Bake for 25 minutes or until the potatoes begin to brown. Remove to a cooling rack, and sprinkle with cheese and scallions; cool for at least 15 minutes before serving.

MEAT FILLING INGREDIENTS

1 tablespoon **vegetable oil**

1½ pounds **ground beef**

½ large **onion**, peeled and diced

1 cup **peas**

1 cup **carrots**, diced

⅛ cup **garlic**, minced

1 cup **Guinness stout**

1 cup **dry red wine**

1 cup strong **beef broth**

2 teaspoons dried **basil**

2 teaspoons dried **oregano**

2 teaspoons dried **sage**

Salt and freshly ground **black pepper** to taste

SAINTLY MEAL *for* MARCH

ST. JOSEPH

A Hearty Italian Meal

Minestra di Lenticchie e Riso
Lentil and Rice Soup

Pasta con le Sarde
Sardines in Tomato Sauce with Pasta

Mudrica di San Giuseppe
St. Joseph's Day Bread Crumbs

Bread Crosses

Zeppole di San Giuseppe
St. Joseph's Day Fritters

Struffoli
Honey Balls

ST. JOSEPH

— Protector of the Holy Family —

MARCH 19

Born:	Died:	Patron saint of workers and of the sick
circa 90 B.C.	circa A.D. 18	

Born in Bethlehem in the state of Palestine, St. Joseph is a mysterious figure in Christian history. All that is recorded about the husband of Mary and the foster father of Jesus comes from several references in the Gospels of St. Matthew, St. Luke, and St. John. There is no mention of his age, but some speculate that he was rather elderly when he became betrothed to Mary and that he died when Jesus was a young man. That might explain why so little is known about him.

St. Joseph was visited in a dream by an angel, who told him not to be afraid to marry his betrothed, Mary, who was with child, and he immediately took her as his wife. Possibly two years later, after the birth of Jesus and the visit of the Magi in Bethlehem, St. Joseph received a second

angelic visit. In that, the angel warned St. Joseph that he and his family were in danger because of Herod's intention to massacre the infants of Bethlehem. He was told that he should flee for their safety. Disposing of all their goods, he took Mary and Jesus to Egypt.

When the family returned, St. Joseph moved them into the small town of Nazareth, where he felt safe with his wife and child. Renowned as a humble man of faith who was obedient to God, St. Joseph apparently worked as a carpenter, later teaching his foster son, Jesus, carpentry skills. The final mention of St. Joseph in the Gospels occurs with the Passover visit to the Temple in Jerusalem when Jesus was twelve years old. Joseph and Mary, realizing that their son was not with them on their way back to Nazareth, had to return to Jerusalem to find Him. In no other biblical accounts after this event is St. Joseph mentioned—not at Jesus' death or His Resurrection.

Veneration of St. Joseph began in the year 800, after which devotions to St. Joseph continued to grow. Since the tenth century, March 19 has been recognized as St. Joseph's Day, a solemn feast day in the Western Church.

In 1870, Pope Pius IX declared St. Joseph the patron and the protector of the Catholic Church. In an encyclical in 1889, Pope Leo XIII urged Catholics to pray to St. Joseph. In 1955, Pope Pius XII declared May 1 the feast of St. Joseph the Worker. And in 1989, Pope St. John Paul II presented a plan that ties St. Joseph to the paths of redemption.

St. Joseph is venerated as the model of fathers.

St. Joseph's Table—A Venerated Italian Tradition

The husband of Jesus' mother, Mary, and the foster father of Jesus, St. Joseph is a revered figure in Christian history. In particular, for many Italians and Italian Americans, St. Joseph is one of the most beloved saints. To honor him for his role as the patron of workers and of the family, Italians in Sicily initiated the tradition of St. Joseph's Table, or St. Joseph's Altar, on March 19. The food served for the occasion represents the harvest and incorporates religious elements, such as the breadsticks shaped like crosses.

SHOPPING LIST

BAKING SUPPLIES

All-purpose flour	4 cups + 1 tablespoon
Baking powder	3 teaspoons
Confectioners' sugar	1 cup
Honey	2 cups
Sugar, granulated	3 cups

BREAD

Bread crumbs, unseasoned	2 cups

CANNED GOODS

Anchovies	3
Beef broth	1 cup
Chicken broth	6 cups
Plum tomatoes	1 ½ cups
Sardines	6

CONDIMENTS

Olive oil, preferably extra virgin	¾ cup
Vegetable oil for deep-frying	1 bottle, medium

DAIRY

Butter, unsalted	5 tablespoons
Eggs, large	8
Romano cheese, grated	2 cups
Whole milk	2 ¼ cups

DRY GOODS

Lentils, uncooked	½ cup
Linguini, dry	1 pound
Pine nuts	2 cups
Raisins	1 ¼ cups
Short grain rice (Arborio)	2 cups

FRESH PRODUCE

Carrots, chopped	1 cup
Celery, chopped	1 cup
Garlic	1 head
Italian parsley	1 bunch
Onions, chopped	1 cup
Orange	1 large
Tomato, crushed	4 tablespoons

MEAT

Pancetta, diced	¼ cup

MISCELLANEOUS

Fruit brandy (optional)	2 tablespoons
Nonpareils for garnish	1 package
Pizza dough, prepared	1 package

SPICES

Salt	pinch
Vanilla extract	2 ¼ teaspoons

Minestra di Lenticchie e Riso

Lentil and Rice Soup

INGREDIENTS

SERVES 6 TO 8

½ cup **uncooked lentils**, rinsed in cold water

¼ cup **pancetta**, diced (see note)

1 tablespoon **olive oil**, preferably extra virgin

1 tablespoon **unsalted butter**

2 cloves **garlic**, minced

¼ cup **Italian parsley**, minced

6 cups **chicken broth**

1½ cups canned **plum tomatoes**, coarsely chopped

1 cup **short-grain rice**, such as Arborio

1 cup **carrots**, chopped

1 cup **onions**, chopped

1 cup **celery**, chopped

Grated **Romano cheese** for sprinkling

Lentils are popular in many parts of the world and particularly in Italy, where home cooks turn lentils into soups or stews. Lentils are also popular on the Italian New Year's Day table because they are thought of as good luck omens; this comes from the custom of giving a *scarsella* (purse) full of lentils at the end of the year in the hope that each lentil would turn into a coin, making the recipient one lucky and rich person. This filling lentil-and-rice soup can be made in less than an hour and needs only a salad to provide a complete, well-balanced meal.

1. Pour the lentils into a soup pot. Cover them with cold water, and cook them over medium heat for about 20 minutes or until tender. Drain the lentils, and set aside. In the same pot, stir in the pancetta, and cook over medium heat for 6 to 8 minutes or until crispy. Remove from the pot, and set aside.

2. Add the olive oil and butter, and cook over medium heat until the butter is melted. Stir in the garlic and parsley, and cook until the garlic softens; do not let it turn brown. Stir in the broth, the tomatoes with their juice, the rice, and the chopped vegetables. Bring the mixture to a boil.

3. Reduce the heat to low; cover the pot, and continue cooking until the rice is tender, about 25 minutes. Stir in the lentils, and reheat the soup. Serve immediately, and pass the grated cheese to sprinkle on top.

Pancetta is a flavorful Italian bacon made from pork belly meat. Although it is cured, it should not be eaten raw.

Pasta con le Sarde

Sardines in Tomato Sauce with Pasta

Sardines derived their name from the Italian island of Sardinia, where schools of sardines once filled local waters. Considered a supremely healthful fish packed with protein and vital nutrients, sardines are more readily available canned rather than fresh. For canned sardines, buy the large cans, and select those that are packed in olive oil. If you do find fresh sardines, select those that have no odor and are firm to the touch. To store them before cooking, rinse them in cold water, wrap them in plastic, and place them in a bowl of ice cubes. Substitute one pound of fresh sardine fillets. Add them to the skillet along with the garlic.

1. Heat a skillet over medium heat, add 6 tablespoons of olive oil, the garlic, and fresh sardine fillets (if using), and sauté slowly. As the garlic begins to darken, add the pine nuts, raisins, and canned sardines, and continue cooking for 2 minutes or until the sardines fall apart. Add the crushed tomatoes and the broth, and stir to combine. Increase the heat to medium, and cook for 3 minutes. The sauce should be quite thick, like tomato sauce. Add water if it needs thinning.

2. Meanwhile, cook the pasta in boiling salted water according to the package instructions. Drain, and mix with the sauce. Serve sprinkled with St. Joseph's Day Bread Crumbs.

INGREDIENTS

SERVES 6

6 tablespoons **olive oil** plus extra for the bread crumbs

4 cloves **garlic**, peeled and very finely sliced

2 cups **pine nuts**

1 cup **raisins**

6 **sardines**

1 cup **beef broth**

4 tablespoons **crushed tomatoes**

1 ¾ cups **bread crumbs** (see bread crumb recipe below)

1 pound dried **linguine**

Mudrica di San Giuseppe

St. Joseph's Day Bread Crumbs

The bread crumbs symbolize the sawdust associated with St. Joseph's work as a carpenter. These bread crumbs are a substitute for grated cheese.

Heat the olive oil in a skillet over low heat. Add the bread crumbs, and cook, stirring constantly, until they turn light golden. Stir in the anchovies, and mix well to incorporate them into the bread crumbs. Remove from the heat, cool on paper towels, and sprinkle with the sugar.

INGREDIENTS

MAKES 2 CUPS

1 teaspoon **olive oil**

2 cups fresh **unseasoned bread crumbs**

3 **anchovies**, minced

1 teaspoon **sugar**

Bread Crosses

The simplest way to make the bread crosses is to use prepared pizza dough, cut into small pieces, braided to make crosses, and then brushed with an egg wash and baked at 425 degrees for 12 to 15 minutes.

Zeppole di San Giuseppe

St. Joseph's Day Fritters

These fritters are traditional sweets—made originally in Sicily, according to legends—to honor St. Joseph. La Festa di San Giuseppe is a special day that began in the Middle Ages. A severe drought ended after citizens prayed to St. Joseph, promising him that if he sent rain to end the drought, they would honor him with his own feast day.

1. Bring the milk to a boil in a saucepan over medium heat. Stir in the rice, sugar, vanilla, and salt. Cover the pan, reduce the heat to low, and cook for about 30 minutes or until the rice is cooked and has absorbed the milk. Cool the rice for several hours or overnight.

2. In a skillet toast the pine nuts without oil over medium-low heat until they start to turn a golden brown. Remove from the heat, and set aside to cool. Mix the rice thoroughly with the eggs, raisins, pine nuts, brandy (if using), flour, baking powder, and orange zest.

3. Heat the oil to 375 degrees for deep-frying. Drop 1 tablespoon of the mixture at a time into the oil, and fry until golden brown. You can cook a few at a time, keeping them separate. Drain them on paper towels, and sprinkle with confectioners' sugar.

INGREDIENTS

SERVES 6 TO 8

2 ¼ cups **whole milk**

1 cup uncooked **short-grain rice**

¼ cup **sugar**

¼ teaspoon **vanilla extract**

Pinch **salt**

3 tablespoons **pine nuts**

2 large **eggs**

3 tablespoons **golden raisins**

2 tablespoons **fruit brandy** (optional)

1 tablespoon **all-purpose flour**

1 teaspoon **baking powder**

Grated zest of 1 large **orange**

Vegetable oil for deep-frying

Confectioners' sugar

Struffoli

Honey Balls

Honey balls, or *struffoli*, originated in ancient Greece, but Italy's Neapolitan cooks embraced the recipe centuries ago. Traditionally considered a Christmas special, thanks to an order of Italian nuns, struffoli are enjoyed now elsewhere and all year long. Originally, the marble-size balls were coated with honey, sprinkled with nonpareils, and stacked to resemble a Christmas tree. But these are often just served hot or warm on a platter.

1. Combine the sugar and butter in a large mixing bowl. Using an electric mixer on medium speed, blend together until the mixture is light and fluffy, 5 to 8 minutes. Scrape down the sides of the bowl as needed. Beat in the eggs, one at a time, blending well after each addition. Add the flour gradually, beating well; add the baking powder and vanilla, and continue beating until a soft dough is formed. If the dough is too sticky, sprinkle in more flour until it does not stick.

2. Divide the dough into 8 equal pieces. Roll each piece on a lightly floured board into a long, pencil-thin rope. Then cut each rope into ½-inch pieces. Using your palms, lightly roll the pieces into small balls.

3. Heat the oil to 350 degrees. Line a sheet pan with paper towels. Fry about 12 pieces of dough at a time. Cook until golden brown all over. Remove with a slotted spoon and place on the towels to drain. Repeat until all the dough is cooked. Cool, and reserve the fried dough in a large bowl.

4. Combine the sugar and water in a saucepan. Cook over low heat, and stir until the sugar is completely dissolved. Add the honey. Continue to stir until the mixture reaches a simmer. Pour the mixture over the fried dough balls. Toss the balls gently to coat them well.

INGREDIENTS

SERVES 10 TO 12

FOR THE HONEY BALLS

1 cup **sugar**

4 tablespoons **unsalted butter**, at room temperature

5 **large eggs**

4 cups **all-purpose flour**

2 teaspoons **vanilla extract**

2 teaspoons **baking powder**

Nonpareils for garnish

FOR THE HONEY SYRUP

½ cup **sugar**

½ cup **water**

2 cups **honey**

FOR FRYING

6 to 8 cups **vegetable oil**

A Prayer to
ST. JOSEPH

O Blessed Saint Joseph, faithful guardian and
protector of virgins, to whom God entrusted
Jesus and Mary, I implore you by the love which
you did bear them, to preserve me from every
defilement of soul and body, that I may always
serve them in holiness and purity of love. Amen.

—Used with permission from Catholic.org

MARCH 27

ST. JOHN OF EGYPT

— *Egypt* —

Born: circa 305, Died: circa 394

St. John of Egypt spent his youth
training as a carpenter with his
father. Upon receiving a calling from
the Holy Spirit, he went into the
desert to live an ascetic life, traveling
to different monasteries. At age forty,
he moved to the top of a cliff for
isolation.

There St. John carved out three
small cells, leaving little openings
through which he could receive food
and advise those seeking spiritual
guidance. Reportedly, he had the gift
of prophecy, which may explain why
he was sought out by so many.

Foreseeing his death, St. John
received no visitors for three days.
He died peacefully in the position of
prayer.

BASBOUSA

A POPULAR EGYPTIAN SWEET CAKE, basbousa (also spelled *basboosa*) has many names throughout neighboring countries from the Middle East to the Balkans to the Horn of Africa. The word roughly translates as "my sweet," and the Egyptian Coptic Christians enjoy this cake for Lenten and Advent season fasts.

This recipe was donated by Amira Ibrahim, who suggested using coarse semolina. She noted that it is generally served with hot tea or coffee and may be topped with heavy cream.

1. Preheat the oven to 350 degrees. Grease a 9 x 13-inch baking pan, and set aside.

2. Melt the butter, and let it cool to room temperature. Combine the sugar and yogurt in a large mixing bowl. Stir in the coconut, baking powder, baking soda, and vanilla extract, and mix until well combined. Add the semolina and butter. Mix well. Pour the mixture into the prepared pan; sprinkle nuts over the top, if desired.

3. Bake the cake for 40 to 50 minutes or until golden brown and a tester inserted in the center of the cake comes out clean.

4. Meanwhile, prepare the syrup by combining the sugar and water in a saucepan. Cook over medium heat, stirring, and after the sugar dissolves, add the lemon juice and bring the mixture to a boil; cook for 5 minutes. Reduce the heat to very low, and continue cooking for 20 to 25 minutes. Remove from the heat, and let it cool slightly; it will thicken while cooling. If it hardens before the cake is ready, simply reheat it when the cake comes out of the oven. While the cake and the syrup are hot, pour the syrup over the cake, and let it set for 15 minutes.

INGREDIENTS

SERVES 8 TO 10

CAKE

½ cup **unsalted butter**

1 cup **sugar**, or less as desired

1 cup **plain yogurt**

¾ cup finely shredded **coconut**

½ teaspoon **baking powder**

½ teaspoon **baking soda**

Dash **vanilla extract**

1 ½ cups **coarse semolina**

Nuts for sprinkling

SYRUP

1 cup **sugar**

1 cup **water**

1 teaspoon **lemon juice**

APRIL

APRIL 1

ST. MARY OF EGYPT

— Egypt —

Born: circa 344, Died: circa 421

St. Mary of Egypt lived a sinful life in Alexandria as a beggar and a prostitute. Joining a pilgrimage to Palestine, she paid her way by offering her services to others. In Jerusalem, she continued her dissolute ways until she attempted to enter the Church of the Holy Sepulchre and an unseen force barred her. St. Mary realized that her sins prevented her entrance.

Approaching a nearby icon of Our Lady, she asked forgiveness and begged to be allowed into the church. If allowed entry, St. Mary promised to repent and live as a hermit in the wilderness. She was granted entry, and the next morning, she set out for the Palestinian desert, where she lived alone for forty-seven years.

SHORBET ADS
Egyptian Yellow Lentil Soup

One of Egypt's oldest crops, lentils were first cultivated in about 600 B.C. on the banks of the river Nile. The use of lentils appears in the book of Genesis (25:29-34), when Esau returned home and asked his twin brother, Jacob, to give him a bowl of cooked lentils. Jacob agreed, but only if Esau would give him his birthright, which was the title of his inheritance.

1. Put the lentils into a large stockpot, and cover with 5 cups of stock. Add the tomato, potato, carrot, and salt, and bring to a boil. Reduce the heat to low, and cook for 20 to 30 minutes, skimming any foam off the surface.

2. Meanwhile, heat the oil in a pot over medium-high heat. Add the onion, and sauté for about 2 minutes. Turn the heat to medium low, and cook until golden and caramelized, 8 to 10 minutes. Stir in the cumin and turmeric, and cook for 1 minute. Set aside.

3. Remove the lentil mixture from the heat, and purée in batches in a blender. Add the lentils to the onions and spices; add the remaining 3 cups of stock (if you prefer a thicker soup, add less). Cook the soup over low heat for about 10 minutes or until thickened. Season to taste with salt and pepper. Serve immediately, topped with the parsley or cilantro, and pita chips.

INGREDIENTS

SERVES 4

2 cups dried orange split **lentils**, rinsed in cold water

8 cups low-sodium **stock**, or as needed

1 medium **tomato**, chopped

1 **Yukon gold potato**, peeled and diced

1 **carrot**, peeled and diced

Salt and freshly ground **black pepper** to taste

2 tablespoons **olive oil**

1 large **onion**, peeled and diced

1 teaspoon **cumin**, ground

1 teaspoon **turmeric**, ground

1 tablespoon fresh **parsley** or **cilantro**, chopped, for garnish

Pita chips for garnish

APRIL 5

ST. VINCENT FERRER
— *Spain* —

Born: 1350, Died: 1419

St. Vincent Ferrer came from a well-to-do family in Aragon, Spain. Growing up, he witnessed his family's generosity in helping the poor and the disadvantaged. Historians note that, at eight years old, St. Vincent started fasting on Wednesdays and Fridays. He also assisted at daily Mass, a ritual he described as "the most sublime work of contemplation."

At the age of eighteen, he joined the Dominicans. After several years of intense studies, committing Scripture to memory, he was ordained a priest in Barcelona in 1379. He became one of Catholicism's greatest preachers and converted thousands during his extensive travels throughout Spain and much of Western Europe, including Italy, France, Germany, England, Scotland, and Ireland.

CERDO ADOBADO
Pork in Adobo

THIS ARAGONIAN DISH INCLUDES the traditional seasoning adobo, used in the technique *adobado* to preserve meats, specifically pork. Many Latin countries have their own versions of this seasoning, which may include hot or mild chilis, vinegar, and in the Philippines, soy sauce. But it is likely that Spaniards in Aragon created the original version.

Traditionally, the meat was marinated in the adobo, then fried lightly, covered with oil, and stored in a covered container. Today's cooks marinate the meat for at least one day and up to one week before preparation. Some recipes call for adding vinegar and crushed red pepper to the marinade. Cooks may also use either sweet or hot paprika or both. Various versions of the adobo spice mixture are sold at many supermarkets but are not necessary for this recipe.

1. Combine the oregano, paprika, turmeric, cumin, garlic, and salt in a mixing bowl, and drizzle in the oil until the mixture forms a runny sauce. Adjust the seasonings to taste, keeping the flavors balanced.

2. Place the pork chops in a glass or ceramic dish, and spoon ⅓ of the adobo sauce over the meat to coat it. Turn the chops over and repeat, adding another ⅓ of the sauce. Cover the dish, and refrigerate for at least 24 hours. Save the remaining sauce for the finished meal. If you refrigerate the sauce, the olive oil will likely thicken. Bring the sauce to room temperature before using.

3. Heat a skillet over medium heat, and when hot, add the pork chops and some sauce. Cover the skillet, and cook the pork chops about 4 minutes on each side or until the meat is done (145 degrees). Remove from the skillet, spoon the remaining sauce over the pork chops, and serve.

INGREDIENTS

SERVES 4

3 teaspoons **oregano**, dried

3 teaspoons **paprika**, ground

1 teaspoon **turmeric**, ground

1 teaspoon **cumin**, ground

1 large **garlic clove**, peeled and chopped

Salt to taste

About 1 cup **olive oil**, or as needed

4 **pork chops**, at least 1 inch thick or about 8 ounces each

APRIL 18

ST. APOLLONIUS

— Italy —

Born: early 2nd century, Died: circa 185

St. Apollonius was born in Rome sometime in the early second century. Little is known about his life, except that he was a popular Roman senator who became an ardent Christian, well versed in Scripture. He wrote an *Apologia*, or defense of the Faith, which is still one of the most revered documents of early Christianity.

When the praetorian prefect challenged St. Apollonius to renounce Christ, he refused and was sent to appear before the Senate. There he gave a lengthy discourse on Christianity and Christ's life. For this, the Senate condemned him to death. History is unclear about the exact date and the cause of death: beheading, having his legs crushed, or drowning.

POLENTA CON SALSICCIA E CARCIOFI

Polenta with Sausage and Artichoke Hearts

POPULAR IN NORTHERN AND CENTRAL ITALY, polenta originated probably in the sixteenth century, when the cultivation of corn began in Western Europe. Italians learned to grind the white or yellow kernels coarsely and slow-cook the ground kernels in water or broth. It can then be spooned into a bowl or onto a plate and dressed up with meat, cooked vegetables, cheese, or butter and milk, or eaten plain.

Modern-day cooks have created a faster-cooking version as well as precooked polenta that comes in a tube and needs only reheating by grilling, frying, or baking. Serve this with slices of Italian bread.

1. Heat the oil over medium heat in a large skillet, and fry the polenta slices for 3 to 4 minutes per side or until the slices soften. Remove them from the skillet, and set aside.

2. Add the artichoke slices, onion, red bell pepper, and garlic to the skillet, and cook for about 5 minutes, stirring often. Add more oil as needed. After the onion and red pepper soften, remove the vegetables from the skillet. Add and cook the sausage slices until browned.

3. Put the artichokes, onion, red bell pepper, garlic, and sausage slices into a large saucepan. Stir in the marinara sauce and chopped sun-dried tomatoes. Season the mixture with salt and pepper. Cook over medium heat until the mixture is hot throughout.

4. To serve, arrange a polenta slice on each plate, spoon the artichoke mixture over the polenta, and garnish with the shredded mozzarella. Serve hot.

INGREDIENTS

SERVES 4

2 to 3 tablespoons **olive oil**, or more as needed

Four 2-ounce round slices precooked **polenta**

One 13 ½ ounce can sliced **artichokes**, drained

1 medium **onion**, peeled and diced

1 **red bell pepper**, seeded and diced

3 medium-size **Italian sausages**, sliced

1 ½ cups **marinara sauce**, or more as needed

2 tablespoons **oil-packed sun-dried tomatoes**, chopped, as desired

Salt and freshly ground **black pepper** to taste

2 cups shredded **mozzarella cheese** for garnish

APRIL 21

ST. ANSELM OF CANTERBURY

— Italy —

Born: circa 1033, Died: circa 1109

St. Anselm of Canterbury was a Benedictine abbot and a brilliant theologian. Traveling to England, he met with Father Lanfranc, who was then archbishop of Canterbury. Upon Lanfranc's death, many thought that St. Anselm would be his successor. King William II, however, usurped the position for himself. But after a long illness, the king relented, naming St. Anselm archbishop.

This was a time of tremendous turmoil between Church and state. Two opposing popes, as well as English royalty, fought for the supremacy of the Church. St. Anselm was twice sent into exile for his public stance on the matter. Upon his eventual return, he convinced the English kings to relinquish their inappropriately acquired rights to rule the Church.

CHEDDAR SCONES

MAKES 12 SCONES

THE SCONE HAS A PROUD SCOTTISH AND, LATER, BRITISH HISTORY. The first mention of a scone in literature appeared in the 1500s in Scotland, where scones were originally made with oats. Their formalized acceptance as part of British cuisine came in the mid-1800s. Since then, scones have become a ritual item in afternoon teas.

Scones and biscuits are similar quick breads. Scones may be assembled from wheat, barley, or oats. Baking powder is the leavening agent. Scones may also contain herbs; fruits, such as raisins or dried cranberries; shredded cheese; or chocolate bits. Before baking, the dough is shaped into a large circle and sliced into wedges or cut into squares or circles.

1. Preheat the oven to 450 degrees. Line a baking sheet with parchment paper, and set aside.

2. Combine the flour, baking powder, sugar, baking soda, salt, and dry mustard in a mixing bowl. Add the butter, and using a pastry blender or your fingertips, rub it into the flour until the mixture resembles bread crumbs. Stir in the shredded cheese. Beat together the egg and buttermilk, and quickly stir the mixture into the flour in about 20 seconds. The dough will be somewhat sticky.

3. Place the dough onto a well-floured surface, and knead it very gently about 10 times or just enough to bring it together. Divide the dough in half. With well-floured hands, pat each half into a 6-inch circle about ½ inch thick. Cut each circle into 6 wedges. Place the wedges on the lined baking sheet, and brush the tops with the egg wash.

4. Bake the scones for about 15 minutes or until the tops turn golden. Remove from the oven, and eat hot or warm.

INGREDIENTS

3 cups **all-purpose flour** plus extra for dusting

1 tablespoon **baking powder**

1 tablespoon **sugar**

½ teaspoon **baking soda**

½ teaspoon **salt**

½ teaspoon **dry mustard**

¼ pound (1 stick) cold **unsalted butter**, diced

1 cup grated **extra-sharp Cheddar cheese**

1 **egg**, beaten lightly

1 cup **buttermilk**

1 **egg** beaten with 1 tablespoon **water** or **milk** for egg wash

SAINTLY MEAL *for* APRIL

◡

ST. MARK THE EVANGELIST

A Vegetarian Lebanese Lunch

Mujaddara bi Fasoulia
Pinto Beans and Cracked Wheat

Salat Baladi
Cucumber and Tomato Salad with Mint

Kishk el Foukara
Milk Pudding with Nuts

ST. MARK

— The Evangelist —

APRIL 25

Born:	Died:	Patron saint of Venice and of notaries
Unknown date	circa 68	

The history of St. Mark, born of Jewish parents in Cyrene, is unclear. Not even his birth date is known. But he was evidently the son of Mary of Jerusalem and the cousin of St. Barnabas. His surname was Mark, and his first name, John.

Christian tradition states that he evangelized with St. Paul and St. Barnabas on their trip to Antioch. St. Mark also held close ties to St. Peter, who referred to St. Mark as "his son." Although St. Mark was not one of the Twelve Apostles, he may have attended and been inspired by one of Jesus' public talks. One of the four evangelists, he likely wrote his Gospel, the Gospel according to Mark, between A.D. 60 and 70, based upon what he learned from St. Peter.

He lived in Alexandria, Egypt, for many years, probably as its bishop, and died there as a martyr. He is often depicted holding his Gospel.

SHOPPING LIST

BAKING SUPPLIES

Cornstarch	5 tablespoons
Sugar, granulated	6 tablespoons

CONDIMENTS

Olive oil	½ cup
Red Wine Vinegar (or **Sherry**)	⅓ cup
Vegetable oil or **coconut oil** for deep-frying	⅓ cup

DAIRY

Whole milk	5 cups

DRY GOODS

Almonds, whole, peeled	1 cup
Cracked wheat, coarse	1 cup
Pinto beans, dry	2 ½ cups
Pistachios, peeled	1 cup
Walnuts, whole and shelled	1 cup

PRODUCE

Cucumbers, Persian	4 large
Mint	1 bunch
Onions	2 medium
Onion, red	1 medium
Tomatoes	4 large

MISCELLANEOUS

Orange Blossom Water	2 tablespoons

SPICES

Black Pepper	to taste
Salt	to taste

Mujaddara bi Fasoulia

Pinto Beans and Cracked Wheat

A traditional Lebanese vegetarian dish with the deep, rich flavor of caramelized onions, this should be served with plain yogurt, preferably Greek; a plate of trimmed raw vegetables, such as scallions, radishes, and carrots; and wedges of pita bread. The cook recommends using coarse cracked, or bulgur, wheat (no. 2), if possible.

1. Soak the pinto beans in water overnight. The next day, put the beans in a stockpot, cover them with water, and boil for about 10 minutes. Drain the beans, and cover them with 4 cups of warm water. Bring to a boil again over medium heat.

2. Meanwhile, in a large skillet, heat the vegetable oil over medium heat, and add the onions. Fry the onions for 15 to 20 minutes, stirring occasionally, until they caramelize and become crunchy. Discard the oil, and carefully add 2 cups of water from the pinto beans. Let the onions boil for 10 to 15 minutes or until the water turns a deep caramel color. Combine the onions and the cooking water with the beans, and continue cooking over medium heat for 15 to 20 minutes. Stir in the olive oil, the cracked wheat, and the salt, and cook, stirring often, for about 15 minutes more or until most of the water has boiled away. Serve hot or cold.

INGREDIENTS

SERVES 4 TO 6

2 ½ cups dry **pinto beans**

⅓ cup **vegetable oil** or **coconut oil**

2 medium **onions**, peeled and minced

¼ cup **olive oil**

1 cup **coarse cracked wheat**

½ teaspoon **salt**, or more to taste

Salat Baladi

Country Salad

Celebrating simple ingredients, this salad highlights the flavors of the summer. Persian cucumbers are shorter than their English cousins and sweeter than the American varieties. You can use any variety of tomatoes, quartered beefsteaks or halved cherry tomatoes; both are welcomed here. The addition of mint, *na'na* in Lebanon, gives this a decidedly Mediterranean twist.

In a large bowl, combine the cucumbers, tomatoes, and red onion slices, and mix. Top with the mint, vinegar, and olive oil. Add the sugar, salt, and pepper, and gently toss. Let it sit for about an hour so that the flavors have a chance to come together.

INGREDIENTS

SERVES 6

4 large **Persian cucumbers**, halved and cut into half-inch chunks

4 large ripe **tomatoes**, cut into 1-inch chunks

1 medium **red onion**, halved and thinly sliced

½ cup **fresh mint**, roughly chopped

⅓ cup **sherry** or **red wine vinegar**

¼ cup **olive oil**

1 tablespoon **sugar**

Salt and freshly ground **black pepper** to taste

Kishk el Foukara

Milk Pudding with Nuts

This easy-to-make Lebanese dessert translates into English as "kiosk of the poor" in the mountainous region from which this cook comes. Elsewhere in the country, it is known as *muha-lla-biyyeh*. Its subtle orange flavor adds a hint of mystery. You could buy cracked or minced nuts, but processing them before cooking them yields a stronger flavor. For those who have nut allergies, you may serve the milk pudding topped with raisins and mint. Note: Both almonds and pistachios are sold already peeled at most supermarkets.

1. Process the almonds, pistachios, and walnuts in a food processor for 15 to 20 seconds or until finely chopped. Mix the milk, sugar, and cornstarch in a bowl to dissolve the cornstarch. Heat the mixture in a saucepan over medium-low heat until it begins to boil and starts to thicken, stirring continuously. Add the orange blossom water, and stir for 3 more minutes.

2. While the mixture is still hot, pour half into a 2-inch-deep heatproof serving dish. Sprinkle half the nut mixture over the top. Add the remaining milk mixture, and top it with the rest of the nuts. Let the dish stay at room temperature for 30 minutes, and then refrigerate it for 1 hour prior to serving.

INGREDIENTS

SERVES 8

1 cup peeled **whole almonds**

1 cup peeled **pistachios**

1 cup shelled **whole walnuts**

5 cups **whole milk**

5 tablespoons **sugar**

5 tablespoons **cornstarch**

2 tablespoons **orange blossom water** (mazaher)

Prayer on the
FEAST OF ST. MARK

O God, who raised up Saint Mark, Your Evangelist,
and endowed him with the grace to preach the
Gospel, grant, we pray, that we may so profit from
his teaching as to follow faithfully in the footsteps of
Christ. Who lives and reigns with You in the unity of
the Holy Spirit, one God, for ever and ever. Amen.

—Collect from the Holy Mass on the Feast of St. Mark

APRIL 29

ST. CATHERINE
OF SIENA

— Italy —

Born: 1347, Died: 1380

At age six, St. Catherine of Siena experienced a vision of Christ with three apostles, inspiring her to devote herself to God. As a young woman, she was accepted as a Dominican Tertiary.

In 1366, while St. Catherine was praying, Christ and His Mother appeared to her. Christ placed on St. Catherine's finger a ring that only she could see. She now felt empowered to go out into the world to help others.

St. Catherine spent her life gathering people into the Faith and working with the papacy to reunite a divided Church. She fought against infidels trying to eradicate the Faith and the peace of Italy. She also received the stigmata, invisible to all until her death.

PANFORTE DI SIENA
Italian Christmas Cake

THIS CLASSIC ITALIAN DESSERT was created in the town of Siena between the eleventh and thirteenth centuries. It was originally made for the nobility because the recipe contained pepper, a very rare commodity.

Modern-day bakers have created their own versions, such as this one, which contains cocoa, an ingredient unavailable in Siena centuries ago. This special cake is enjoyed at festive Christmas meals. The ground white pepper adds an unexpected zip. The cook suggests sprinkling the confectioners' sugar through a decorative doily to create a pattern on the cake's top. It is generally served with hot tea or coffee and may be topped with heavy cream.

1. Preheat the oven to 325 degrees. Spray the bottom of a 9-inch springform pan with vegetable oil. Cut a parchment-paper circle, and place it on the bottom of the pan. Spray the sides of the pan and the parchment paper liberally with the vegetable oil. Set aside.

2. Mix the first 8 ingredients in a large mixing bowl, and set aside. In a medium saucepan, heat the sugar and honey over medium-high heat until the sugar is dissolved and the mixture begins to boil; stir the mixture to prevent scorching, and cook for 4 to 5 minutes. Remove from the heat, and stir in the candied fruit mix, the lemon zest, and the extract. Stir in the mixed dry ingredients. Pour the batter into the prepared springform pan, and spread it evenly with a spatula to fill the pan. Place the pan in the oven, with a pan on the rack below to catch any drippings.

3. Bake for 50 to 55 minutes or until the center is set and a cake tester inserted in the center comes out clean. Remove from the oven, and allow to cool completely on a wire rack. Do not remove the springform sides until the cake is completely cool.

4. Invert the springform pan onto a plate, and remove the parchment paper from the bottom of the cake. Turn the panforte upright onto a serving dish, and sift confectioners' sugar over the top. Cut into small wedges, and serve with a steaming cup of espresso or cappuccino.

INGREDIENTS
SERVES 16

1 ¼ cups **dry-roasted almonds**, coarsely chopped

¾ cup **all-purpose flour**

¼ cup **unsweetened cocoa powder**

1 ½ teaspoons **cinnamon**, ground

½ teaspoon **allspice**, ground

⅛ teaspoon **cloves**, ground

⅛ teaspoon **nutmeg**, ground

Pinch **white pepper**, ground

¾ cup granulated **sugar**

¾ cup **honey**

1 ½ cups **candied mixed fruit**

1 teaspoon fresh **lemon zest**

¼ teaspoon **vanilla** or **almond extract**

2 tablespoons **confectioners' sugar**, for sprinkling

MAY

MAY 3

ST. PHILIP THE APOSTLE

—*Israel*—

Born: 5, Died: 80

St. Philip was from Bethsaida, as were the apostles St. Andrew and St. Peter. He was a follower of John the Baptist, and he attended the wedding in Cana. Having become acquainted with Jesus, St. Philip shared the news with his friend Nathanael that he had found the Messiah. Scripture scholars identify Nathanael as the apostle Bartholomew.

After Jesus' death and Resurrection, all the disciples were dispersed to preach the Gospel. According to historical accounts, St. Philip journeyed to Greece, where he was eventually crucified at Hierapolis.

STUFFED GRAPE LEAVES

Many Middle Eastern and Asian cultures prepare dishes using grape leaves. Stuffing grape leaves became a culinary tradition during the reign of Alexander the Great. During Alexander's siege of Thebes, residents ate any bits of meat rolled up in grape leaves to survive.

In ancient Israel, stuffing grape leaves for Rosh Hashanah tallied with the Sephardic tradition of offering stuffed vegetables for the feast. Even today, the stuffed grape leaf symbolizes ancient Israel's cultural traditions.

Note: The meat strips prevent the grape leaves from sticking and also give flavor to the dish. If using dried grape leaves, these must be softened in boiling water for about 30 minutes. Serve with pita bread and yogurt.

1. Remove the rolled-up grape leaves from the jar and separate them carefully. Discard the brine. Rinse each leaf under cold water, and pat them dry between paper towels. Line the bottom of a large pot with meat strips.

2. Mix together the ground meat, rice, butter, 1 teaspoon salt, and black pepper in a large bowl. Using a teaspoon, place some of the mixture onto the middle of a grape leaf. Spread the mixture evenly, leaving about ¼-inch space from the edge at each end of the leaf—this will make folding the leaf easier. Fold from the stem end of the leaf; tuck in the empty sides toward the center; and keep folding to roll up the leaf completely. Repeat with the remaining ingredients. Set the leaves aside.

3. Start laying the rolled grape leaves over the meat strips in the bottom of the pot, keeping them close together. Repeat, layering the leaves, until the pot is three-quarters full. Pour the water or broth over the top layer; add the remaining salt. Cover the leaves with a heatproof plate to keep them in place.

4. Cover the pot with a heatproof lid, and cook over medium heat for 30 minutes. Add the lemon juice. Reduce the heat to low, and cook for another 40 minutes. Remove from the heat, and let stand for 15 to 20 minutes. Serve hot.

INGREDIENTS

SERVES 4 TO 6

One 1-pound jar **grape leaves** in brine

3 or 4 strips marbled **beef** or **lamb**, about 1 pound

1 pound ground **beef** or **lamb**

1 cup rinsed **long-grain rice**

2 tablespoons **unsalted butter**

1 tablespoon **garlic**, minced

2 teaspoons **salt**

½ teaspoon ground **black pepper**

2 cups **water** or **beef broth**, or more as needed

½ to 1 cup **lemon juice**

MAY 10

ST. DAMIEN OF MOLOKAI

— *Belgium* —

Born: 1840, Died: 1889

❦

St. Damien of Molokai followed three of his siblings into the religious life. When his older brother fell ill and could not fulfill his directive to move to Hawaii, St. Damien went in his place.

In 1866, the government established a leper colony on the island of Molokai. The lepers sent there needed medical and spiritual care, so St. Damien volunteered to go. He discovered a lawless colony filled with disease and immorality. St. Damien took on the roles of doctor and spiritual director and organized a work force to create housing, orphanages, and sources of food and water. In 1884, St. Damien found that he had contracted leprosy but refused to leave for treatment.

CARBONNADE WITH ENDIVE AU GRATIN

CARBONNADE IS A RICH BEEF STEW made with onions and beer and is a very popular dish in Belgium. The traditional recipe calls for beef cheeks, but you can substitute any inexpensive, tough cut of beef that will tenderize after simmering in a flavorful liquid over low heat for several hours. Serve this with crispy fries and mayonnaise. The secret ingredient, Belgian Speculoos cookies, helps thicken the sauce.

FOR THE CARBONNADE

Heat the butter in a large deep-dish Dutch oven or another saucepan over medium heat. Add the meat and onions to the saucepan, and fry them until the onions start to brown. Reduce the heat to low, and pour in the beer. Stir in the crumbled cookies, the mustard, and the salt and pepper. Cover, and cook for about 2 hours or until the meat is cooked. It should remain firm but tender.

Serve with crispy fries with mayonnaise and endive au gratin (see next page).

Beef cheeks can be tough to come by, so if they are not readily available, you can substitute another beef cut, such as a chuck roast.

If you can't find Speculoos cookies, you can try using gingerbread cookies or another hard spice cookie.

CARBONNADE INGREDIENTS

SERVES 6

4 tablespoons **unsalted butter**, or more as needed

4 pounds **beef cheeks**, cut into 1-inch cubes (see note)

2 **onions**, peeled and minced

One 11.5-ounce bottle **Belgian brown ale**

On 8.8-ounce package **Speculoos Belgian spice cookies**, crumbled (see note)

3 tablespoons **Dijon mustard**

Salt and freshly ground **black pepper** to taste

FOR THE BELGIAN ENDIVE AU GRATIN

A head of Belgian endive grows to about 6 inches long with white leaves that taper upward to pale green-yellow. Crispy Belgian endive is often served raw in salads. It is also cooked and served as a side dish or as part of an entrée. The vegetable originated in Belgium and is also popular in France and the Netherlands. Belgian cooks often serve it wrapped in ham, but this family has chosen bacon instead.

1. Preheat the oven to 350 degrees. Grease a deep baking dish large enough to hold the wrapped endives and sauce. Set aside.

2. Trim off the white stem end of each head of endive, and cut it in half lengthwise. Using a sharp knife, remove the bitter inner core of each half. In a large saucepan, melt the ¼ cup butter over medium heat. Add the lemon juice and about 1 cup of water. Add the endives, sliced sides down, and cover; reduce the heat to medium low. Slowly braise the endives until they are tender, 5 to 10 minutes, depending on size. Remove from the pan and set aside. Drain any leftover liquid.

3. Melt the 2 tablespoons of butter in the same pan over medium-low heat. Whisk in the flour, and stir continuously until the mixture becomes a golden paste. Slowly add the milk, continuously stirring, until it becomes smooth. Stir in 1½ cups of grated Gruyère cheese, the nutmeg, and salt and pepper. Cook the sauce over low heat, stirring frequently, for 5 to 8 minutes more or until smooth. Remove from the heat.

4. Wrap each endive half in a slice of bacon (or ham), and place all of them in the prepared baking dish. Cover them with the cheese sauce, and sprinkle the remaining Gruyère on top. Sprinkle with the bread crumbs, if desired.

5. Bake for 25 to 30 minutes or until the sauce bubbles and the cheese on top turns a golden brown. Remove from the oven. Garnish with the chopped parsley, and serve immediately.

BELGIAN ENDIVE AU GRATIN INGREDIENTS
SERVES 4 TO 6

8 heads **Belgian endive**, washed and trimmed

¼ cup plus 2 tablespoons **unsalted butter**

Juice of 1 **lemon**

About 1 cup **water**

2 tablespoons **all-purpose flour**

1½ cups **whole milk**

2 cups finely grated **Gruyère cheese**, divided

¼ teaspoon **nutmeg**, ground, or more to taste

Salt and freshly ground **black pepper** to taste

16 slices thick **bacon** or **ham**

Unseasoned **bread crumbs** (optional)

¼ cup **fresh parsley**, chopped, for garnish

SAINTLY MEAL

for

MAY

ST. ISIDORE THE FARMER

A Farm Dinner

Bacon-Wrapped Beef Medallions

Portobello Mushroom Gravy

Garlic and Cheese Mashed Potatoes

Zucchini and Yellow Squash Piccata

Strawberries with Crème Fraîche

ST. ISIDORE

— The Farmer —

MAY 15

Born:	Died:	Patron saint of Madrid and of farmers
circa 1070	1130	

San Isidro Labrador, or St. Isidore the Farmer, was born in Spain into a devout and humble family. As a youngster, he served as a laborer for the Madrid-based landowner, John de Vergas, for whom he worked for the remainder of his life. But what set St. Isidore apart from his fellow laborers was his profound religious beliefs. His coworkers complained to their master that St. Isidore turned up late for work. Every morning, St. Isidore went to an early Mass at a nearby church. When de Vergas looked into the complaints—so the legend goes—he found an angel at the plow until St. Isidore's prayers at church ended. Legends also relate that St. Isidore continued to recite prayers while tilling the fields.

As many as four hundred miracles have been attributed to St. Isidore. Many indicate how he interacted with angels. The miracles often pointed to his charitable character. For example, one of his most notable acts was feeding the starving pigeons from his supply of wheat grains. He emptied out half his bag to feed the birds, but God miraculously refilled the bag. St. Isidore is remembered for his devotion to the poor and to animals.

St. Isidore was beatified in 1619 by Pope Paul V and canonized in 1622 with four other Spanish Catholic Fathers. St. Isidore is the patron saint of the Catholic Rural Life organization, formerly called the National Rural Life Conference.

SHOPPING LIST

BAKING SUPPLIES

Cornstarch — 1 to 2 tablespoons

Sugar, granulated — 2 to 3 tablespoons

CANNED GOODS

Beef stock — 1 ½ cups

Chicken broth or white wine — ¼ cup

CONDIMENTS

Olive oil — ½ cup

Organic beef bouillon concentrate — 1 tablespoon

Worcestershire sauce — ¼ cup

DAIRY

Butter, unsalted — 3 tablespoons

Cheddar cheese, grated — 1 cup

Crème fraîche — 2 cups

Heavy cream — 1 ½ cups

Whole milk — 2 tablespoons plus

PRODUCE

Baby Portobello mushrooms — 1 pound

Garlic — 2 cloves

Onions — 1 small, 1 large

Parsley — 1 bunch

Potatoes, Yukon gold — 2

Strawberries — 3 pints

Tomato — 1

Yellow squash — 2

Zucchini — 2

MEAT

Applewood-smoked bacon — 6 slices

Beef tenderloin — about 3 pounds or 6 two-inch (8-ounce) medallions cut from the tenderloin

MISCELLANEOUS

Merlot (optional) — ½ cup

Toothpicks — 6

SPICES

Black pepper — to taste

Rosemary, ground — pinch

Sage, ground — pinch

Salt — to taste

Thyme, ground — pinch

Bacon-Wrapped Beef Medallions

Many farm dinners have gained the reputation of being wholesome, filling, and countryish. But sometimes farmers elevate their main meal into something that can be elegant and worthy of a high-end feast. This meal was created by a farming family in rural Virginia, and their menu will appeal even to sophisticated city dwellers.

1. Cut the tenderloin crosswise into 2-inch-thick medallions. Wrap each medallion in bacon, and pin each slice to the meat with a toothpick. Combine the olive oil and Worcestershire sauce in a large stainless-steel pan, and place the medallions in the marinade. Marinate the meat overnight.

2. Preheat the oven to a low broil setting; place the racks midway below the broiler.

3. Remove the medallions from the marinade, lay them on a broiler pan, and place them in the oven for 5 minutes. Remove, turn the meat over, and broil for 3 more minutes. Check for desired doneness.

INGREDIENTS

SERVES 6

6 **beef medallions**, about 8 ounces each, cut from the tenderloin

6 slices **Applewood-smoked bacon**

¼ cup **Worcestershire sauce**

¼ cup **olive oil**

Toothpicks

Portobello Mushroom Gravy

Thinly slice the portobello mushrooms, and set aside. Heat the oil in a large skillet, and sauté the onion over medium heat until translucent. Add the mushrooms, beef stock, Merlot (if using), bouillon concentrate, and meat drippings. Continue to cook and stir over medium heat. Blend the cream and the cornstarch together, and stir this mixture into the gravy. Continue cooking and stirring until the mixture thickens. Season with salt and pepper to taste.

INGREDIENTS

1 pound **baby portobello mushrooms**

2 tablespoons **olive oil**

1 small **onion**, peeled and diced

1½ cups **beef stock**

½ cup **Merlot wine** (optional)

1 tablespoon organic **beef bouillon concentrate**

Meat drippings from **steak**

1 cup **heavy cream**

1 to 2 tablespoons **cornstarch** to thicken gravy

Salt and freshly ground **black pepper** to taste

Garlic and Cheese Mashed Potatoes

1. Put the potatoes into a large saucepan, and add the salt. Cover the potatoes with water, bring to a boil over medium heat, and reduce the heat to low. Cook covered for 20 minutes or until fork tender.

2. Meanwhile, warm the cream and butter together. Drain the water from the potatoes, return the pot to the burner, and steam off any remaining water. Put the potatoes into a bowl, add the cream, butter, and garlic, and mash with a potato masher. Stir in the cheese, milk, and salt and pepper, using a wooden spoon.

INGREDIENTS

SERVES 6

2 pounds **Yukon gold potatoes**, peeled and quartered lengthwise

½ teaspoon **salt**

6 tablespoons **heavy cream**

3 tablespoons **unsalted butter**

2 cloves **garlic**, peeled and minced or finely grated

1 cup grated **cheddar cheese**

2 tablespoons **whole milk**, or more as needed to smooth the potatoes

Salt and freshly ground **black pepper** to taste

Zucchini and Yellow Squash Piccata

Heat the oil in a large skillet over medium heat, and sauté the onion until translucent. Add the zucchini, yellow squash, and tomato, and stir well. Add enough chicken broth or white wine to help steam the vegetables until tender. Stir in the parsley, sage, rosemary, thyme, and salt and pepper. Serve hot or at room temperature.

INGREDIENTS

SERVES 4 TO 6

2 tablespoons **olive oil**

1 large **onion**, peeled and diced

2 **zucchini**, cubed

2 **yellow squash**, cubed

1 **tomato**, chopped

About ¼ cup **chicken broth** or **white wine** to steam squash

¼ cup **parsley**, chopped

Pinch **sage**

Pinch **rosemary**

Pinch **thyme**

Salt and freshly ground **black pepper** to taste

Crème Fraîche

You can buy ready-made crème fraîche or make your own by combining 2 cups of heavy cream with 4 tablespoons of buttermilk. Put the mixture in the refrigerator in a glass container for 8 to 24 hours until thickened. Keep refrigerated until ready to use.

Strawberries with Crème Fraîche

Rinse the berries, and sprinkle with sugar. Serve with crème fraîche.

INGREDIENTS

SERVES 6

3 pints **strawberries**, stemmed

2 to 3 tablespoons **sugar**

2 cups **crème fraîche**

A Prayer to
ST. ISIDORE

Almighty God and Father of all, You give to man the opportunity to harvest the good things of Your creation and to build up Your Kingdom. By the prayers and holy example of St. Isidore, inspire us to be diligent in our laboring and to have trustful hearts that rely totally on Your loving providence. Help us to care for creation and use it for its highest good; to bring true charity to those around us. Through the intercession of Your faithful servant St. Isidore, help all who sow and reap to abound in rich harvests. May all who work the land be treated fairly and be allowed to share in the fruits of their labor. We ask this through our Lord Jesus Christ, Your Son, who lives and reigns with You and the Holy Spirit, one God, for ever and ever. Amen.

—Courtesy of Pedro de la Cruz
© 2017 at CatholicPrayerCards.org

MAY 16

ST. SIMON STOCK

— England —

Born: 1165, Died: 1265

As superior general of his Carmelite Order, St. Simon Stock founded many Carmelite communities in cities such as Cambridge and Oxford and throughout France and Italy as well. His dedication transformed the Carmelites into a mendicant order.

In 1251, Our Lady appeared to St. Simon, offering him a brown scapular. She told him that whosoever dies wearing it will avoid eternal damnation. Although Catholic historians cannot validate this apparition, the brown scapular—the large ones made of two woolen squares attached by cords and the small ones made of two small squares often decorated with pictures, also attached by cords—is worn by all Carmelites today. They may also be worn by laypersons.

PORK CHOPS WITH APPLE-MUSHROOM SAUCE

THIS BRITISH RECIPE MAKES a fitting entrée for celebrating St. Simon Stock's feast.
It is typically served with mashed potatoes and seasonal vegetables.

1. Heat the olive oil in a saucepan large enough to hold the 4 pork chops. Season the pork chops on both sides with salt and pepper. Heat the oil over medium-high heat. Panfry the chops quickly on both sides until browned. Remove from the pan, and set aside.

2. In the same pan, melt the butter, and add the mushrooms, apple, onion, garlic, thyme, rosemary, and sage. Cover the pan and cook over medium-high heat for 5 to 10 minutes. Pour in the apple juice, and let it cook, uncovered, until the liquid is reduced by half, about 15 minutes. Add the vegetable broth, and cook to reduce the liquid by half again, about 10 minutes.

3. Reduce the heat to medium low. Gradually add the heavy cream, stirring constantly. When well combined, return the pork chops to the pan. Cook for 6 to 8 more minutes until the pork chops are done. Remove from the heat, season to taste, and serve.

INGREDIENTS

SERVES 4

4 **pork chops**

Salt and freshly ground **black pepper** to taste

1 to 2 tablespoons **olive oil**

1 tablespoon **unsalted butter**

6 to 8 ounces **mushrooms**, trimmed and sliced

1 **Granny Smith apple**, peeled and chopped finely or grated

1 medium **onion**, peeled and chopped

2 to 4 cloves **garlic**, peeled

1 tablespoon fresh **thyme**, finely chopped

1 tablespoon fresh **rosemary**, finely chopped

½ teaspoon **sage**, ground

1½ cups **apple juice**

1 cup **vegetable broth**

¼ cup **heavy cream**

MAY 30

ST. JOAN OF ARC

— *France* —

Born: 1412, Died: 1431

At age thirteen, St. Joan of Arc received messages from St. Michael, St. Catherine, and St. Margaret. They foretold events in France and what her role would be: to assist King Charles VII, whose military situation in Orléans was desperate.

The king deemed St. Joan fit to lead his troops, and after her three-month military campaign, Britain declared defeat. But future conflicts awaited her.

When the Duke of Burgundy attacked Paris, St. Joan was injured and captured. She was put on trial, falsely accused of many crimes, and condemned to be burned at the stake. In her last hours, St. Joan embraced a cross and called out the name of Jesus.

GATEAU DE CRÊPES
Crêpes Cake

BORN IN ORLÉANS, FRANCE, Chef Arnaud Herodet spent his childhood living in French Polynesia, where his father worked for the military. As a young adult, Herodet returned to France to attend a culinary school in Vichy, after which he worked in numerous hotels in Europe as a chef. Herodet returned to French Polynesia, where he worked for four years in the Hotel Kia Ora on the island of Rangiroa. There, he was assigned to create and produce elegant pastries every day.

That hotel experience proved to be the foundation for his later work experience in the United States. He moved to Washington, D.C., in 1992 and eventually became the chef at the French embassy. He noted that this delicate cake originated in Vichy, where he made it daily in a one-star Michelin restaurant.

1. Combine the egg yolks, sugar, flour, and vanilla extract in a large mixing bowl, mixing well. Combine the milk and butter in a saucepan, and cook over medium heat until it boils. Remove from the heat, and allow to cool slightly. Slowly stir the hot milk mixture into the egg mixture, blending well.

2. In a large mixing bowl, using an electric mixer, beat the egg whites and the pinch of sugar until stiff. Gently fold the whites into the egg-sugar mixture. Heat a 7-inch nonstick crêpe pan over medium-low heat, and add about 2 teaspoons of butter. When the butter starts to sizzle, add about 3 tablespoons of batter to the pan, swirl the batter around, and cook the crêpe slowly. When it puffs up and turns golden, slip it out of the pan onto a plate, and sprinkle it with a little sugar. Repeat until there are 5 crêpes; some batter will remain.

3. Heat a 12-inch nonstick skillet over medium-low heat, and add about 1 tablespoon of butter. When the butter starts to sizzle, swirl in the remaining batter, and cook it until it puffs and turns golden. Slip it out of the skillet onto the stacked crêpes. Cool the skillet, and put it upside down on top of the crêpe stack to deflate it. Slice, and serve while hot. If desired, you may top the cake with various small berries of your choice, such as strawberries, blueberries, or raspberries.

INGREDIENTS
SERVES 4

8 large **eggs**, separated, at room temperature

6 tablespoons **sugar** plus 1 pinch

¾ cup plus 2 tablespoons **all-purpose flour**

1 teaspoon **vanilla extract**

1 cup **milk**

6 tablespoons **unsalted butter** plus extra for cooking

Fresh **strawberries, blueberries,** or **raspberries** for topping (optional)

JUNE

JUNE 1

ST. JUSTIN MARTYR

—— Palestine (of Greek ancestry) ——

Born: 100, Died: 165

St. Justin was born in Palestine to pagan Greek parents. He spent his youth studying the works of Greek philosophers. By chance, he met a stranger who spoke to him about Christian philosophy. Afterward, St. Justin embraced Christianity, immersing himself in Holy Scripture. He began to evangelize, hoping to convert pagans.

St. Justin's pathway took him to Rome, where he spent many years writing several works on the Faith. In his second *Apology*, he foresaw his persecution and martyrdom, naming the Roman cynic who would eventually pursue him and see him killed. When asked to denounce his Faith, St. Justin replied, "No one who is rightly minded turns from true belief to false."

KOLOKITHOKEFTEDES
Zucchini Fritters

THIS SIMPLE RECIPE, which may have originated in Crete, comes together quickly. It calls for a Greek cheese, kefalotiri. Also spelled *kefalotyri*, it is a hard, salty white cheese made of unpasteurized sheep or goat's milk. Substitutes for kefalotiri are equal amounts of grated Parmesan or Romano. The fritters can also be baked. Serve these as a first course or as a vegetable side dish. Top each serving with plain yogurt or tzatziki sauce, which is available at many grocery stores and online.

1. Grate the zucchini, and sprinkle the shreds with salt. Place them in a colander, and squeeze them to drain the excess liquid. Set aside for 30 minutes, and then squeeze again.

2. Mix the remaining ingredients together. Stir in the zucchini shreds, and form the mixture into 16 small patties, about ½ inch thick and 3 inches in diameter. Refrigerate them for at least 20 minutes. Heat the oil in a large skillet over medium-high heat. Lightly flour each patty, and fry them until golden on both sides. Remove from the oil, and drain on paper towels. Serve hot.

INGREDIENTS
SERVES 6 TO 8

3 to 4 large **zucchini**

1¼ teaspoons **salt**

2 large **eggs**, lightly beaten

½ cup **all-purpose flour** plus extra for dusting patties

½ cup grated **kasseri cheese**

½ cup grated **manchego cheese**

½ cup grated **kefalotiri cheese**

¼ cup sliced **scallions** or chopped **chives**

¼ teaspoon freshly ground **black pepper**

About ¼ cup **olive oil** for frying

Plain yogurt for serving

Tzatziki, if desired

JUNE 9

ST. EPHREM THE SYRIAN

— *Turkey* —

Born: 306, Died: circa 373

St. Ephrem the Syrian—also Ephraem or Ephraim—was born in Nisibis, Mesopotamia (modern-day Turkey). At the age of eighteen, he was baptized into the Faith by St. James of Nisibis. He became a devout follower and defender of Christ. As a poet and teacher, he wrote numerous Christian poems and hymns.

After relocating to Edessa with many of his Christian followers, he founded a theological school. He earned a reputation as a homilist and a staunch enemy of the ten or more heresies raging in Edessa. He was ordained a deacon but declined to become a priest. A simple and holy man, St. Ephrem preferred living in a small cave above the city.

KIFTA
Syrian Beef Meatloaf

THROUGHOUT THE CENTURIES, SYRIAN CUISINE HAS EVOLVED around numerous vegetables accompanied by lamb and prepared with olive oil, spices, and assorted beans, nuts, and grains. Today, cooks may substitute beef for lamb and pair that with vegetables. The word *kifta*, also known as *kafta* and *kofta*, refers to ground meat shaped into a meatloaf.

1. Preheat the oven to 350 degrees. Spray a large baking pan with nonstick spray, and set aside.

2. In a large mixing bowl, combine the beef and cubed onions, and season the mixture with salt and pepper. Put the sliced potatoes on the bottom of the pan. Spread the meat mixture on top, and cover with the sliced tomatoes.

3. Bake for 40 minutes or until the meat and potatoes are cooked through. Remove from the oven, and serve hot.

INGREDIENTS

SERVES 6 TO 8

2 tablespoons **vegetable oil**

2 pounds **ground beef**

2 large **onions**, peeled and cubed

4 medium **potatoes**, peeled and sliced

6 **plum tomatoes**

Salt and freshly ground **black pepper** to taste

JUNE 21

ST. ALOYSIUS GONZAGA

—— *Italy* ——

Born: 1568, Died: 1591

St. Aloysius Gonzaga showed extraordinary piety during his childhood, reciting numerous psalms and practicing many devotions. Although his noble family had other plans for him, he became a Jesuit priest, inspired by accounts of Jesuit missionaries in India.

In Rome, he entered the novitiate and came under the spiritual direction of St. Robert Bellarmine. St. Aloysius took his vows in 1587, the same year a plague broke out in Rome.

With his fellow Jesuits, he tended to the sick and the dying in the streets and in the hospitals, washing and feeding them. Being in such close contact with plague victims, St. Aloysius contracted the disease. He died at the age of twenty-three.

MINESTRONE

MAKES 3 QUARTS

ONE OF ITALY'S OLDEST DISHES, the vegetable-rich minestrone soup—which may be embellished with meat—could predate the expansion of Rome into an empire. Such a soup was mentioned in Marcus Apicius's cookbook, *De re coquinaria*, written in the fourth or fifth century A.D.

Through the ages, the basic recipe has remained fairly standard and includes onions, tomatoes, beans, and a soup stock. There is no set or established recipe, however. Making minestrone really depends on what seasonal vegetables the cook has on hand.

The chef suggests making this in large batches and freezing some to enjoy at other mealtimes. Only add the garnishes each time you plan to serve the soup.

1. Heat the olive oil in a medium-size stockpot over medium heat. Add the carrots, celery, and onion, and cook for 8 to 10 minutes or until the onion is translucent. Add the garlic, and cook for 5 minutes more, stirring occasionally. Add the cabbage, stirring well, and cook for another 5 minutes. Add the dried herbs, and mix well. Add the beans and water, bring to a boil over medium-high heat, and reduce the heat to low. Add the tomatoes and squash or sweet potatoes, and cook for another 10 to 15 minutes or until the squash is soft but not mushy. Season with salt and pepper.

2. Remove from the heat. Add the lemon juice and the spinach or kale. Garnish with fresh basil leaves and Parmesan cheese. Serve hot.

INGREDIENTS

SERVES 4 TO 6

3 tablespoons **olive oil**

2 large **carrots**, peeled and sliced

2 stalks **celery**, sliced

1 medium **onion**, peeled and diced

2 or 3 cloves **garlic**, peeled and minced

¼ head **white cabbage**, coarsely chopped

Pinch dried **basil** or another dried herb

One 14-ounce can **cannellini** or **navy beans**, drained

1½ to 2 quarts filtered or regular **water**

One 14-ounce can diced **tomatoes**

1 cup cubed **butternut squash** or **sweet potatoes**

Salt and freshly ground **black pepper** to taste

1 to 2 tablespoons **lemon juice**

½ cup **spinach** or **kale**, chopped, for garnish

Fresh **basil leaves** for garnish

Grated **Parmesan cheese** for garnish

JUNE 24

ST. JOHN THE BAPTIST

— *Israel* —

Born: circa 5 B.C., Died: circa A.D. 31

St. John the Baptist elicits a popular image of a scraggly, bearded man carrying a staff and dressed in a camel's hair garment. He lived in the wilderness, subsisted on locusts and honey, and traveled from village to village as a prophet. He warned people to repent of their sins, and he baptized them.

Sometime after baptizing Jesus in the Jordan River, St. John was arrested and imprisoned by the ruler of Galilee, Herod Antipas. Herod was angry because St. John had denounced his marriage to Herodias, the divorced wife of Herod's half-brother. By Jewish law, the marriage was illegal. At Herodias's request, Herod ordered St. John's beheading.

ST. JOHN THE BAPTIST HONEY CAKE

HISTORICAL ACCOUNTS OF HOW ST. JOHN THE BAPTIST LIVED in the wilderness tell of his surviving on a diet of locusts and honey. Obviously, not many home cooks today would serve a dessert of honey-drenched locusts, but this rich honey cake will be a witness to part of St. John's diet. A Bundt pan and one 8 x 4-inch loaf pan or three 8 x 4-inch loaf pans work equally well. Note that different sized pans affect the baking time. Wrapping the cooled cakes in foil will keep them good for several days.

1. Preheat the oven to 350 degrees. Lightly spray a Bundt pan and one 8 x 4-inch loaf pan, or three 8 x 4-inch loaf pans, with non-stick spray. Sprinkle them with flour, and set aside.

2. Combine all the dry ingredients in a large mixing bowl, and stir them together until well combined. In a separate bowl, beat together the vegetable oil, honey, coffee, eggs, orange juice, and brandy (if using). Make a well in the center of the dry ingredients, and add the liquid ingredients, whisking together until well combined.

3. Pour the mixture into the prepared pans, filling them only two-thirds full. Set the pans on top of a large baking sheet, and place in the oven.

4. Bake for 40 to 50 minutes or until a tester inserted in the center comes out clean. Remove the pans from the oven, and let them sit for 15 minutes before removing the cakes from the pans. Turn them out onto cooling racks to cool completely.

INGREDIENTS
SERVES 10 TO 12

3 ½ cups **all-purpose flour**

1 ½ cups **granulated sugar**

1 tablespoon **cinnamon**, ground

1 teaspoon **baking powder**

1 teaspoon **baking soda**

½ teaspoon **salt**

½ teaspoon **cloves**, ground

½ teaspoon **allspice**, ground

1 cup **vegetable oil**

1 cup **honey**

1 cup strongly brewed **coffee**

3 large **eggs**, well beaten

½ cup **orange juice**, preferably fresh

½ cup **brown sugar**

¼ cup **whiskey**, **brandy**, or **orange liqueur** (optional)

SAINTLY MEAL *for* JUNE

ST. JOSEMARÍA ESCRIVÁ

A Spanish Menu

Gazpacho
Cold Tomato and Vegetable Soup

Paella
Spanish Rice with Pork

Crema Catalana

Strawberries with Sugar and Vinegar

ST. JOSEMARÍA ESCRIVÁ

JUNE 26

Born: 1902	Died: 1974	Patron saint of those with diabetes

Born in Barbastro, Spain, into a devout Catholic family, St. Josemaría Escrivá de Balaguer y Albás felt even as a youngster that God was calling him to do something important in life. Unsure of his ultimate goals, he decided to enter the priesthood, studying in Logroño and in Zaragoza. He was ordained a priest in March 1925. After serving a brief stint in a rural church, he headed to Madrid to study law at the Central University.

In 1928, St. Josemaría's life took a dramatic turn, though he did not realize its future impact. During a prayer retreat, he believed that God sent him this message: he "saw" Opus Dei (Work of God), an apostolate within the Catholic Church by which all Catholics—lay and ordained—could perform secular work to sanctify themselves before God. This would be a way for all Catholics to find holiness in daily activities and to find a deeper love for God and their fellow men. St. Josemaría then devoted his time to forming this mission. In 1930, he started Opus Dei's work with women and youth. He spent the first few years focused on those who were sick or living in slums in Madrid.

In 1934, St. Josemaría had the first edition of his most famous work, *The Way*, published (under the original title, *Spiritual Considerations*). He later expanded and revised it. It has subsequently been translated into numerous languages with more than 4.5 million copies printed. St. Josemaría also wrote *Holy Rosary*, *The Way of the Cross*, and *Christ Is Passing By*, among other spiritual works.

When the Spanish Civil War broke out in 1936, St. Josemaría fled from Madrid to the city of Burgos. He was persecuted, but unlike other priests, he survived the war, returning to Madrid when the war ended in 1939. He finished his studies and received a doctorate in law from the University of Madrid. At the request of local bishops, St. Josemaría traveled throughout Spain speaking to priests and eventually to laity about the spiritual concepts of Opus Dei.

In 1943, St. Josemaría was given approval for the founding of the Priestly Society of the Holy Cross. The society has many objectives, including the ordination of priests in Opus Dei and the spiritual growth of diocesan priests, who may be a part of the society yet remain clergy in their own parishes.

Because he understood that Opus Dei had a mission with the universal Church, St. Josemaría moved to Rome in 1946 to have easy access to the Holy See. Not only did the Holy See openly praise the work of Opus Dei, but St. Josemaría also started taking Opus Dei throughout Italy, Great Britain, and Portugal. After receiving provisional approval from Pope Pius XII in 1947, for the next three years Opus Dei did apostolic work throughout France, Ireland, Central Europe, Mexico, and the United States. In 1950,

Pope Pius XII gave the final approval to St. Josemaría, enabling him to take the Opus Dei message to Germany and Latin America.

For the next twenty-five years until his death, St. Josemaría not only took the message and the work of Opus Dei to numerous countries, but he also earned a doctorate in theology from the Lateran University in Rome. He was appointed consultor to the Pontifical Commission for the Authentic Interpretation of the Code of Canon Law, among his many other achievements.

His legacy has left an indelible impression on the Catholic world. Bishop Eijo y Garay wrote in 1941 to the Jesuit provincial of Toledo: "Fr. Escrivá is an exemplary priest, chosen by God for apostolic enterprises; humble, prudent, self-sacrificing in work, docile to his bishop, of outstanding intelligence and with a very solid spiritual and doctrinal formation."

St. Josemaría Escrivá was beatified in 1992 by Pope St. John Paul II, who then canonized him in 2002.

SHOPPING LIST

BAKING SUPPLIES

Cornstarch	2 tablespoons
Sugar, granulated	2 cups

BREAD

French bread	1 loaf

CANNED GOODS

Beans, white	one 15-ounce can
Chicken stock	2 cups
Fish stock	1 cup
Peas	1 cup

CONDIMENTS

Cider vinegar	1 tablespoon
Olive oil	2 cups plus
Thai fish sauce	1 tablespoon
Wine vinegar	several tablespoons to taste

DAIRY

Eggs	4 large
Whole milk	2 ¼ cups

DRY GOODS

Rice, short grain	3 cups

PRODUCE

Cucumber	1
Eggplant	1 large
Figs (optional)	several, to taste
Garlic	1 head
Green beans	1 cup
Green bell peppers	3
Lemons	3
Onions, white	1 ½
Onion, red	½
Orange	1
Parsley	1 bunch
Red bell peppers	2
Scallions	2
Strawberries	4 pounds plus for garnish
Tomatoes	4 or 5
Tomatoes, Italian	4

MEAT

Chicken thighs	8
Chorizo	½ pound
Pork chops	2 large boneless, at least 1 inch thick and weighing 8 ounces or more

MISCELLANEOUS

White wine	½ cup
Toothpicks	6

SEAFOOD

Clams, shell on	1 pound
Shrimp	24 large

SPICES

Bay leaves	2
Black pepper	to taste
Cinnamon stick	1
Nutmeg, ground	pinch
Rosemary, ground	1 tablespoon
Saffron	1 teaspoon
Salt	to taste
Thyme, ground	½ teaspoon

Gazpacho

Cold Tomato and Vegetable Soup

This classic cold Spanish soup, which many believe originated in Andalusia, traces its origins to ancient Roman times. The soup's name may have devolved from Greek, Israeli, Latin, or Moorish cooks. Regardless of its source, gazpacho has become a must-have summer dish. It has varying characteristics, as some recipes use fruits instead of vegetables as its base. Whatever the ingredients, one Andalusian source said: "*De gazpacho no hay empacho* [There's never too much gazpacho]."

Traditionally assembled from finely hand-chopped tomatoes, cucumbers, and green peppers, the soup now comes together in seconds, thanks to the food processor or blender. The quantities are only an approximation, because you should sample the soup and add ingredients to suit your taste. Using already chilled vegetables lets you eat a cold soup right away. Classic gazpacho showcases summer-ripe produce and can become an entire meal in itself with plenty of bread and wine. Otherwise, serve it with a Spanish pasta entrée and a delicate citrus dessert.

Combine tomatoes, cucumber, onion, green pepper, garlic, olive oil, vinegar, salt, and pepper in a food processor or blender, and pulse until mixture is smooth. Pour the soup into serving bowls, and garnish with scallions, green peppers, and bread cubes.

INGREDIENTS

SERVES 4

4 or 5 whole ripe **tomatoes**, stem end removed and quartered

1 **cucumber**, peeled and sliced

1 **onion**, peeled and chopped

1 **green pepper**, seeded and chopped

3 cloves **garlic**, peeled and chopped

2 to 3 tablespoons **olive oil**, or more as needed

1 tablespoon **cider vinegar**

Salt and freshly ground **black pepper** to taste

Scallions, chopped, for garnish

Green peppers, cubed, for garnish

Bread cubes for garnish

Paella

Spanish Rice with Pork

Paella is claimed to have originated in Valencia, Spain, in the mid-nineteenth century, but it has much older roots. The name *paella* may be derived from an old French or Latin word for "pan," a flat-rimmed shallow pan that cooks over direct heat. For small portions, a 6-inch round pan suffices, but to feed 12 to 15 people, the cook needs a 30-inch round pan. Such large pans require a large burner or a special propane paella burner. Alternatively, the cook can use an electric countertop cooker.

Many Latin countries have devised their own versions of this rice-based dish. The traditional paella's basic ingredients include a short-grain rice, preferably Spanish; vegetables; legumes; and meat, such as rabbit, chicken, or duck. Over time, some cooks have introduced seafood as the main meat. Today's cooks also use different kinds of rice, even the flavorful, long-grain Thai jasmine rice.

The following recipe is separated into three parts: the marinade, the paella, and the stock.

 You can substitute a large stainless steel or aluminum skillet for the paella pan. Cast iron and nonstick pans are discouraged. Experts like thin carbon steel pans because they heat quickly and don't retain much heat.

INGREDIENTS

SERVES 8 TO 10

MARINADE

Juice of 2 **lemons**

1 cup **olive oil**, or more as needed

2 to 4 cloves of **garlic**, peeled and minced

About ½ teaspoon **saffron**

Salt and freshly ground **black pepper** to taste

PAELLA

8 **chicken thighs**

24 large **shrimp**, peeled and deveined

1 **red bell pepper**, cut in half lengthwise and seeded

¼ cup **olive oil**, or more as needed

1 large **eggplant**, trimmed, quartered, and thinly sliced

2 large (at least 8-ounce) boneless **pork chops**, cubed

1 tablespoon **rosemary**, ground

Salt and freshly ground **black pepper** to taste

1 **red bell pepper**, seeded and cubed

1 **green bell pepper**, seeded and cubed

½ large **white onion**, peeled and cubed

½ large **red onion**, peeled and cubed

4 **Italian tomatoes**, cubed

½ pound **chorizo**, thinly sliced

3 cups **short-grain rice**

1 cup trimmed **green beans**, cut into 1-inch pieces

One 15-ounce can **white beans**, drained

1 pound **clams**, shells on

1 cup **peas**

2 tablespoons fresh **parsley**, chopped

STOCK

2 cups **chicken stock**

1 cup **fish stock**

½ cup **white wine**

1 tablespoon **Thai fish sauce**

2 **bay leaves**

½ teaspoon **thyme**, ground

½ teaspoon **saffron**

Pinch **nutmeg**, ground

1.   Prepare the marinade for the chicken and shrimp: Combine the juice of 2 lemons with 1 cup of olive oil. Season with garlic, salt, pepper, and saffron. Mix the marinade well. Coat the chicken and shrimp on all sides, and set aside.

2.   Preheat the oven to 400 degrees. Roast the two red pepper halves skin side up, and cook until the skin starts to char. Remove from the oven, and set aside. When cool, run under cold water, and rub the skin off. Cut into slices, and set aside for decoration.

3.   In the paella pan, heat ¼ cup of olive oil over medium heat, and add the eggplant slices. Sauté until the slices are golden on both sides, about 10 minutes. Remove the eggplant from the pan, and set aside for decoration. Season the cubed pork with salt, pepper, and rosemary.

4.   Sauté the marinated chicken in the paella pan until browned. Set aside. Sauté the shrimp for 2 to 3 minutes. Set aside.

5.   Add 2 cups of water to a large stockpot. Bring the water to a boil, add the pork cubes, and cook until the meat is done, about 10 minutes. Remove the meat, and set aside, reserving the cooking water for the final stock. To the cooking liquid from the pork, add the chicken stock, white wine, fish stock, fish sauce, bay leaves, ground thyme, saffron, and ground nutmeg. Add salt and pepper to taste. Bring to a boil over medium heat, and cook for 5 minutes.

6.   To the remaining liquid in the paella pan, add the cubed red and green peppers, the onion, and cubed tomatoes, and sauté until softened, about 5 minutes. Add more olive oil, if needed. Add the sliced chorizo, the pork, green beans, white beans, and rice. Stir well.

7.   Level the rice mixture, and quickly arrange the 8 chicken thighs, the shrimp, clams, slices of eggplant, and roasted red pepper strips on top of the rice. Pour the prepared stock evenly over the entire paella, and sprinkle with parsley and peas.

8.   Cover tightly with aluminum foil, reduce the heat to medium-low, and cook for 30 minutes or until the rice is tender. Check frequently during the last ten minutes of cooking. When the rice is almost done, remove the pan from the heat, and let rest. The rice will absorb the remaining liquid and continue to cook while the bottom layer forms the famous crust called "socarrat."

Crema Catalana

Closely resembling the famous French dessert crème caramel, the Spanish Crema Catalana differs in its use of milk, not heavy cream, and of cornstarch for thickening. In addition, this is not baked in a water bath but is thickened on the stovetop before setting. In Catalonia, it is known as Crema de Sant Josep, for Saint Joseph's Day.

1. Dissolve the cornstarch in a splash of water, and set aside. Pour the milk into a saucepan, and stir in the lemon and orange peels and the cinnamon stick. Heat over medium heat until it begins to boil, stirring constantly. As soon as it boils, reduce the heat to low.

2. Next, using an electric mixer on medium speed, beat the egg yolks with the sugar until the mixture turns a pale yellow, about 3 minutes. Beat in the dissolved cornstarch and a spoonful of the hot milk. Remove the fruit peels and cinnamon stick from the hot milk. Slowly stir in the egg yolk mixture. Keep stirring, to prevent the yolks from scrambling, until the mixture thickens, about 2 minutes.

3. Remove from the heat, and pour the mixture into traditional clay dishes or ramekins. Allow the Crema to cool, and then chill the Crema Catalana for about 4 hours or overnight.

4. To serve, bring the custard to room temperature, and sprinkle the surface evenly with sugar. Caramelize the sugar under a broiler or with a small kitchen blowtorch. Top with fresh fruit, if desired.

INGREDIENTS

SERVES 4 TO 6

2 tablespoons **cornstarch**

2 ¼ cups **whole milk**

1 large slice of **lemon peel**

1 large slice of **orange peel**

1 **cinnamon stick**

4 large **egg yolks**

½ cup plus 2 tablespoons **superfine or regular sugar**

Extra **sugar** for caramelizing the Crema surface

Fresh fruit, such as sliced **figs** or **strawberries**, for garnish (optional)

Strawberries with Sugar and Vinegar

This simple, tasty Spanish dessert is a classic and would pair well with the rich Crema Catalana. See the recipe above.

Slice the strawberries in half, and place them in a large bowl. Add several tablespoons of sugar to taste and a dash of vinegar. Toss gently to coat all the berries. Cover and refrigerate the berries until chilled. Serve cold.

INGREDIENTS

4 pounds fresh **strawberries**, rinsed and hulled

Granulated **sugar** to taste

Wine vinegar to taste

A Prayer to
THE HOLY SPIRIT

Come, O Holy Spirit!

Enlighten my mind to know Your commands;

strengthen my heart against the snares
of the enemy; inflame my will....

I have heard Your voice, and I don't want to harden
myself and resist, saying "Later ... tomorrow."

Nunc coepi! Now I begin! In case
there is no tomorrow for me.

O Spirit of truth and wisdom, Spirit of
understanding and counsel, Spirit of joy and peace!

I want whatever You want. I want because
You want; I want however You want; I
want whenever You want. Amen.

—St. Josemaría Escrivá

JULY

JULY 1

ST. JUNÍPERO SERRA

—*Mexico*—

Born: 1713, Died: 1784

St. Junípero Serra was a Spanish priest who became a missionary to the New World, sailing to Vera Cruz, Mexico. After six months spent at a missionary college in Mexico City, he volunteered to become a missionary to an Indian tribe and for the next two decades opened numerous missions throughout Mexico. On July 1, 1769, St. Junípero arrived in San Diego, California. From 1769 until 1782, he opened nine missions on the California coast, from San Diego to San Francisco.

St. Junípero is referred to as the "Father of California" and the "Apostle of California." He was the first saint to be canonized on American soil.

JERICALLA

YIELDS 10 TO 12 INDIVIDUAL CUSTARDS

CONSIDERED BY HISTORIANS AS A TRADITIONAL MISSION FOOD in the early days of California, this custard has flavors reminiscent of both Spanish and Native American cuisines, and its texture resembles that of French crème brûlée. Food historians debate its origins: one source claims that the nuns who created this dish came from the Jerica region in southeast Spain. Another source states that a nun named Jerica in the Guadalajaran kitchen of Hospicio Cabañas, run by Bishop Ruiz Cabañas, created this custard. The recipe surfaced in California around the time the missions were founded.

1. Place the milk, vanilla extract, and cinnamon stick in a medium saucepan, and cook over medium heat, stirring frequently. Once it begins to bubble and simmer around the edges, reduce the heat to low, and cook for 1 to 2 minutes. Remove from the heat, and let it sit until it cools. When it has cooled, remove the cinnamon stick.

2. Preheat the oven to 350 degrees. Prepare a water bath using a roasting pan; add about ½ inch hot water to the pan.

3. In a medium bowl, beat the egg yolks with a fork or whisk until pale yellow and thick, about one minute. Add the sweetened condensed milk in a stream, and beat with the fork or whisk to incorporate. Add the cooled milk mixture, a ladle at a time, incorporating it gently with the fork or whisk. Avoid causing many bubbles.

4. Place 10 ramekins or custard molds in the water bath. Using a ladle, pour the mixture into the ramekins, dividing it evenly among them. Carefully place the roasting pan in the oven.

5. Bake for about 25 minutes or until the custard begins to set. The top should develop a thick layer, but it should not turn crispy or brown. Remove the pan from the oven, and set the ramekins aside to cool. Serve at room temperature, or chill before serving.

INGREDIENTS

SERVES 6

4 cups **whole milk**

2 teaspoons **vanilla extract**

1 stick **cinnamon**, preferably Ceylon, about 2½ inches long

One 14-ounce can **sweetened condensed milk**

10 **egg yolks**

The chef suggests using the egg whites to make an egg-white omelet.

JULY 9

ST. AUGUSTINE ZHAO RONG

— China —

Born: 1746, Died: 1815

St. Augustine was a Chinese soldier who converted to Christianity. As a diocesan priest, he worked in the province of Sichuan. At that time, China did not welcome Catholics, and St. Augustine was eventually arrested and imprisoned for his apostolic work and for his Faith. One source reports that, because of foul conditions in prison, he contracted a disease and died. Another suggests that he was killed.

In all, about thirty thousand Chinese converts to Christianity were martyred between 1648 and 1930. Among them was St. Augustine Zhao Rong and 119 of his Catholic companions.

CANTONESE GINGER BEEF

COUNTLESS RECIPES SHOWCASE SLICES OR CUBES OF BEEF stir-fried with fresh ginger and scallions. This version comes from famed Hong Kong food writer and restaurant reviewer William (Willie) Mark and typifies his style and Cantonese flavors. The idea with stir-fry cooking is to close the surface of the beef up quickly in the hot oil to preserve the tenderness throughout the remaining cooking process. Serve this with cooked rice and stir-fried vegetables.

1. Put the steak cubes in a shallow baking dish. Combine the marinade ingredients, and pour the mixture over the meat. Set aside for 10 minutes or more. Meanwhile, combine the seasoning sauce ingredients, and set aside.

2. Pour 1 cup of oil into a wok or skillet, and heat over medium-high heat. Add the beef cubes, stirring to prevent their sticking together. Cook for 40 seconds or slightly more as needed, remove the beef, and drain off the oil.

3. Pour 1 tablespoon of oil into the wok, and heat over medium-high heat. Add the ginger and scallions, and stir-fry for about 30 seconds. Return the beef to the wok, and stir-fry for 30 seconds. Remove the wok from the heat. Pour the seasoning sauce over the beef, and stir-fry over medium-high heat. When the sauce comes to a boil, remove the wok from the heat. Serve immediately.

The cooking time in this recipe applies to a wok and might need to be adjusted to add more time when using a skillet.

MEAT & MARINADE INGREDIENTS

12 ounces **sirloin steak**, trimmed of fat and cubed

6 thin slices fresh **ginger**

3 **scallions**, cut into 2-inch lengths

1 cup plus 1 tablespoon **vegetable oil**, preferably **peanut oil**, or more as needed

1 **egg white**

1 tablespoon **Chinese yellow wine** or **Mirin**

1 tablespoon **light soy sauce**

1 tablespoon **cornstarch**

1 teaspoon **sesame oil**

SEASONING SAUCE INGREDIENTS

6 tablespoons **chicken stock**

1 tablespoon **oyster sauce**

2 teaspoons **light soy sauce**

2 teaspoons **cornstarch**

1 teaspoon **dark soy sauce**

JULY 12

ST. VERONICA

—*Israel*—

The details of St. Veronica's life, including the dates of her birth and her death, are largely unknown. But historians note that she lived in Jerusalem at the time of Christ's Passion. She has become a Catholic icon because she rushed to wipe the sweat and blood from Jesus' face with her veil as He struggled to carry the Cross to Calvary. As a result of this act of charity, Jesus' face was imprinted on Veronica's veil, making it one of the most treasured relics of the Catholic Church.

ISRAELI TAHINI COOKIES

YIELDS ABOUT 5 DOZEN

TAHINI PASTE IS MADE OF GROUND SESAME SEEDS and is a popular condiment in not only Middle Eastern, but also North African, Indian, Chinese, and Southeast Asian cuisines. Mixed with other ingredients, such as garbanzos, garlic, honey, and even cocoa, you can make savory and sweet accompaniments. Tahini paste is readily available at well-stocked markets. These sweet, nutty cookies add a note of delight to any dessert offering or a relaxing cup of afternoon tea.

1. Preheat the oven to 325 degrees. Line 2 baking sheets with parchment paper, and set aside.

2. Beat the sugar and butter together in a mixing bowl using an electric mixer on medium speed. Add the tahini and the vanilla extract, and beat again. Combine the flour and the baking powder; stir into the tahini mixture.

3. Form the dough into walnut-size balls. The dough is dry and crumbly, so squeeze it together to make the balls. If it won't stick at all, try adding water, a little at a time, up to ⅓ of a cup. Place the balls on the baking sheets, and gently push a few pine nuts into the top of each for decoration. If the cookie crumbles slightly, just squeeze it back into shape with your fingertips. Repeat with the remaining dough.

4. Bake for 13 to 15 minutes. Do not bake longer. The cookies need a little moisture to retain their shape and not crumble. Cool the baking sheet on a rack, and don't touch the cookies for at least 5 minutes. If they're handled while hot, they will fall apart. Dust with confectioners' sugar when cool, if you wish.

INGREDIENTS

SERVES 4 TO 6

1 cup **sugar**

8 ounces (½ cup) **unsalted butter,** at room temperature

1 cup **tahini**

2 teaspoons **vanilla extract**

2 cups plus 4 tablespoons **all-purpose flour**

1 teaspoon **baking powder**

Up to ⅓ cup **water** to shape dough

Pine nuts for sprinkling

Confectioners' sugar for dusting

Due to its high oil content, tahini, especially raw versions, should be stored in the refrigerator.

SAINTLY MEAL *for* JULY

ST. KATERI
A Native American Lunch

An authentic tribal meal using indigenous ingredients, it represents the healthful and simple diet Native American tribes must have enjoyed. These recipes come from Father Maurice Henry Sands, the first Native American priest from the Detroit area and a member of the Ojibway/Ottawa/Potawatomi tribes.

Anishinaabe Mandaaminaabo
Indian Corn Soup

Zhiiwaagamizigan Gibozigan Okosimaan
Maple Syrup-Baked Squash

Gibozigan Bakwezhigan
Native American Oven-Baked Bread

Mishiimin Wishkobibakwezhigan
Apple Cobbler

ST. KATERI TEKAKWITHA

— Lily of the Mohawks —

JULY 14

Born:	Died:	Patron saint of
1656	1680	Native Americans

Born in the Mohawk village of Ossernenon, near Lake Ontario, St. Kateri Tekakwitha—known as the "Lily of the Mohawks"—led a life filled with much pain and suffering. Yet she worked diligently to help others in need. When she was only four years old, she contracted smallpox when an epidemic struck her tribe, killing her family, including her Christian mother. The disease left St. Kateri partially blind and left her skin scarred.

She was raised by an uncle, the chief of a Mohawk clan. She learned about the Faith through Jesuit missionaries who came to her village. When she turned nineteen, St. Kateri converted to Catholicism on Easter Sunday, taking the name Kateri, the Mohawk version of Catherine, in memory of St. Catherine of Siena.

Members of her tribe resented her conversion, so St. Kateri moved to a Christian Indian village many miles away. There she led a devout life, spending much of her time in prayer. Five years after her conversion, she became ill and passed away at age twenty-four.

St. Kateri Tekakwitha was beatified in 1980 by Pope St. John Paul II and canonized in 2012 by Pope Benedict XVI. She is the first Native American to be recognized as a saint by the Catholic Church.

SHOPPING LIST

BAKING SUPPLIES

All-purpose flour	4 cups
Baking powder	1 ½ tablespoons
Brown sugar	½ cup (packed)
Maple syrup darker variety (look for grade B, or a dark amber)	6 tablespoons
Oats, old-fashioned (not quick cooking)	½ cup
Sugar, granulated	¼ cup

CANNED GOODS

Chicken stock homemade or canned	2 quarts
Navy or kidney beans canned/cooked	2 cups
Indian corn (mandaamin) or canned hominy	4 cups

MEAT

Chicken breast halves bone-in and skin on	2

MILK AND DAIRY

Milk	¾ cup
Butter, unsalted	½ cup (1 stick)

PRODUCE

Acorn squash (okosimaan)	3
Apples, tart	4
Celery	3 large stalks
Onion	1 medium to large

SPICES

Cinnamon, ground

Salt

Black pepper

Anishinaabe Mandaaminaabo

Indian Corn Soup

This comforting soup calls for a traditional Native American corn called *mandaamin*, which in the Algonquin language means "wonder seed." It is also spelled *mandamin*, *mondamin*, or *mondawmin*. Because these kernels are difficult to find, home cooks may use hominy—a treated corn kernel that is soft—as a substitute.

Combine the chicken stock, corn, and beans in a saucepan, and cook over medium heat until the mixture comes to a boil. Stir in the chicken, onions, and celery, and season with salt and pepper. Reduce the heat to low, and continue cooking for about 1 hour or until all the flavors have blended. Serve hot.

INGREDIENTS

SERVES 6 TO 8

2 quarts homemade or canned **chicken stock**

4 cups **mandaamin** (Indian corn), or canned **hominy**, drained

2 cups cooked **navy** or **kidney beans**

2 **chicken breast halves**, cooked, skinned, and shredded

1 cup **onions**, diced

1 cup **celery**, diced

Salt and freshly ground **black pepper** to taste

Zhiiwaagamizigan Gibozigan Okosimaan

Maple Syrup Baked Squash

Indigenous to North and South America, the acorn squash was completely unknown to Europeans until they began to explore the New World. Native Americans introduced European settlers to this hearty winter squash, which was one of their "three sisters"—corn, beans, and squash—important for their survival. For consumers today, picking the best acorn squash means looking for one with a smattering of orange on its nonshiny skin and picking one that weighs less than three pounds.

1. Preheat the oven to 375 degrees. Fill a baking pan large enough to hold the 6 squash halves with ½ inch of water.

2. Slice a very thin section off the bottom of each squash half. This prevents them from tipping during baking. Place the six acorn squash halves skin side down in the baking pan. Wrap the pan with foil to seal it.

INGREDIENTS

SERVES 6

3 **acorn squash**, cut in half lengthwise, seeds removed

2 tablespoons **unsalted butter**

6 tablespoons **maple syrup**

Cinnamon, ground, to taste

3. Bake for about 45 minutes or until the squash is tender. Take the pan out of the oven, and unwrap and discard the foil. Spoon about 1 teaspoon of butter into the center of each squash half. Top each half with 1 tablespoon of maple syrup, and dust with ground cinnamon. Place the unwrapped pan back in the oven for about 10 minutes. Remove, and serve the squash warm.

Gibozigan Bakwezhigan

Native American Oven-Baked Bread

History indicates that most Native American tribes composed a flour-yeast mixture and fried rather than baked their bread. This version of the famous bread calls for no yeast and comes together and bakes quickly.

1. Preheat the oven to 375 degrees. Line a baking sheet with parchment paper.

2. Combine the flour, baking powder, and salt in a mixing bowl, and whisk together until well combined. Make a well in the center of the mixture, and pour in the milk and water. Using a fork, toss together the mixture until it forms a soft, slightly sticky dough; do not overwork the dough.

3. Lightly flour a work surface, and turn the dough onto it. Roll the dough out to form a 1-inch-thick circle. Place the dough on the prepared baking sheet.

4. Bake for about 45 minutes, testing the bread for doneness by tapping it. If baked through, it will sound hollow. Serve warm with butter and honey, if desired.

INGREDIENTS

SERVES 4 TO 6

3 cups **all-purpose flour**, sifted

1 ½ tablespoons **baking powder**

1 teaspoon **salt**

¾ cup **whole milk**

¾ to 1 cup **water**

Butter and **honey** for serving (optional)

Mishiimin Wishkobibakwezhigan

Apple Cobbler

The only native apple is a small, tart crab apple. When making this Native American dessert, select such tart apples as Jonathan, Honey Crisp, or Granny Smith varieties.

1. Preheat the oven to 375 degrees. Coat the bottom and sides of an 8-inch baking dish with baking spray.

2. To make the filling, combine the apples, sugar, flour, and cinnamon. Place the mixture in the baking dish. To make the topping, combine the oats, flour, brown sugar, and butter, mixing well. Sprinkle the topping over the apples.

3. Bake for about 40 minutes or until the topping is golden brown. Remove from the oven, and cool slightly.

INGREDIENTS

SERVES 4

FILLING

4 **tart apples**, peeled and sliced

¼ cup **sugar**

¼ cup **all-purpose flour**

½ teaspoon **cinnamon**, ground

TOPPING

½ cup **old-fashioned oats**

½ cup **all-purpose flour**

½ cup **brown sugar**

¼ cup chilled **butter**, cut into pea-size pieces

A Prayer to

ST. KATERI TEKAKWITHA

Blessed Kateri, you are revered as the mystic of the American wilderness. Though orphaned at the age of four, and left with a scarred face and damaged eyesight from illness, you were esteemed among the Mohawk tribe.

When you asked to be baptized a Christian you subjected yourself to abuse by your people and were forced to run away.

You endured many trials but still flowered in prayer and holiness, dedicating yourself totally to Christ. I ask you to be my spiritual guide along my journey through life.

Through your intercession, I pray that I may always be loyal to my Faith in all things. Amen.

JULY 31

ST. IGNATIUS OF LOYOLA

— Spain —

Born: 1491; Died: 1556

St. Ignatius of Loyola entered the army at age seventeen, and in 1521, a cannonball damaged his legs. During his convalescence from surgeries, he read books on the lives of Christ and of the saints. Profoundly impacted, St. Ignatius went on a pilgrimage after his recovery and confessed his sins. For the next year, he attended daily Mass and spent many hours in prayer. During this year of self-examination, he began writing his famous work, *The Spiritual Exercises*.

In 1534, St. Ignatius and several companions, including St. Francis Xavier and St. Peter Faber, took vows of poverty and chastity. In 1540, with the approval of the pope, these men formed the new Society of Jesus — the Jesuits.

BASQUE LAMB STEW

The Basque country, an autonomous region in Northern Spain, has both a coastal area—the Bay of Biscay—and a mountainous region—the Pyrenees, which separate that part of Northern Spain from the Basque region of France. The population living in the coastal or valley regions are generally fishermen or farmers. But those who live near the Pyrenees are the herders and livestock farmers. Although the majority of animals raised for profit are cattle, sheep come in at a close second. Basque cooks readily infuse their cuisine with ideas and ingredients from others, including the use of olive oil, potatoes, and bell peppers.

1. Heat the oil in a large skillet over medium-high heat. Cook the lamb, without crowding, until all pieces are brown on all sides. Remove with a slotted spoon, and set aside in a large stockpot.

2. Combine the bell peppers, celery, tomatoes, potatoes, onion, and garlic in a large bowl. Cook in batches over medium heat for about 5 minutes, stirring often; the cooking may require more olive oil. Combine the cooked vegetables with the lamb, and scrape the bottom of the skillet to add lamb bits to the stew for flavor.

3. Add 3 cups of stock (or more as needed), the wine, tomato paste, paprika, and bay leaves. Bring the mixture to a boil. Reduce the heat to low, cover, and cook until the lamb is tender, about 1 hour; add the remaining stock, if necessary.

4. Remove the lid, and increase the heat to medium. Discard the bay leaves. Stir in the salt and black pepper to taste. Cook, stirring, until the sauce reduces, about 15 minutes. Adjust the seasonings. Place the stew in a serving dish, and garnish with the chopped parsley. Serve hot.

INGREDIENTS

SERVES 8

½ cup **olive oil**, or more as needed

3 ½ pounds cubed **lamb leg** or **shoulder meat**, preferably American if available

2 **red bell peppers**, seeded and cut into 1-inch cubes

2 **green bell peppers**, seeded and cut into 1-inch cubes

1 ½ **celery stalks**, cut into ½-inch-long pieces

2 **tomatoes**, quartered

2 **potatoes**, peeled and cut into 1-inch cubes

1 large **yellow onion**, peeled and cut into 1-inch cubes

4 **garlic cloves**, peeled and minced

3 to 4 cups **lamb** or **beef stock**

1 ½ cups **white wine**

2 tablespoons **tomato paste**

1 ½ tablespoons **paprika**, ground

2 **bay leaves**

Salt and freshly ground **black pepper** to taste

¼ cup or more fresh **parsley**, chopped

AUGUST

AUGUST 4

ST. JEAN-MARIE VIANNEY

— *France* —

Born: 1786, Died: 1859

From his youth, St. Jean-Baptiste-Marie Vianney saw priests as heroes. When the anticlerical pursuits of the French Revolution began, priests had to preach and practice in secret; therefore, St. Jean-Marie was catechized and received his First Communion privately.

After being ordained in 1815, St. Jean-Marie was assigned to a parish in the small village of Ars. There, his prayers and holy example brought the villagers back to the Faith. St. Jean-Marie was a dedicated priest, often listening to confessions for twelve to sixteen hours a day. Thousands of people traveled from many countries to receive words of love and forgiveness from this simple priest.

POULET A LA NORMANDE
Normandy Chicken

DESPITE ITS MANY VARIATIONS, this chicken recipe highlights two of Normandy's most famous ingredients: apples and apple cider. Most recipes also include heavy cream or crème fraîche, and some include mushrooms. But the basic flavors of apples and apple cider underscore the recipe's Norman roots. Serve in bowls with fresh crusty bread.

1. Heat 2 tablespoons of butter in a large skillet over medium heat. Add enough chicken pieces, skin side down, to cover the base of the pan. Increase the heat to high, and cook the chicken until brown; turn and brown the other side. Remove from the skillet, and repeat with the remaining chicken pieces, as needed.

2. To the same skillet, add 1 tablespoon of butter, the shallots, and the celery, and cook over low heat for 5 minutes. Place the chicken pieces over the vegetables, pour in the cider and stock, and season with salt and freshly ground black pepper. Bring to a boil, reduce the heat to medium low, cover, and cook for 20 minutes or until the juices run clear when a thick piece of chicken is pierced with a sharp knife.

3. Heat the remaining butter in a second large skillet over medium heat until foaming and beginning to turn slightly brown. Add the apples, and fry until lightly colored. Reduce the heat to low, and keep warm. Lift the chicken pieces and vegetables out of their skillet with a slotted spoon, put them in the skillet with the apples, cover, and keep warm. Mix the flour with the crème fraîche to form a smooth paste, whisk into the simmering liquid in the first skillet with the vegetables and broth, bring to a boil, and cook for 3 to 4 minutes. To serve, spoon the sauce over the chicken, and garnish with flat-leaf parsley.

INGREDIENTS

SERVES 4 TO 6

4 tablespoons **unsalted butter**

One 3-pound **roasting chicken**, cut into serving pieces, or 8 **chicken thighs**

6 large **shallots**, peeled and cut in half

4 stalks **celery**, washed and thickly sliced

½ quart **apple cider**

1 cup **chicken stock**

3 red **apples**, cored and sliced into wedges

4 tablespoons **all-purpose flour**

½ cup **crème fraîche**, or ¼ cup **whipping cream** mixed with ¼ cup **sour cream**

Salt and freshly ground **black pepper** to taste

Sprigs of **flat-leaf parsley** for garnish

AUGUST 10

ST. LAWRENCE

— Spain —

Born: 225, Died: 258

St. Lawrence lived in Rome during
the reign of the emperor Valerian,
who persecuted and killed Christians.
St. Lawrence had moved to Rome to
serve under the pope as "the keeper
of the treasures of the Church,"
dispensing alms to the poor and the
needy.

When the prefect of Rome demanded
that St. Lawrence turn over all the
Church's treasures, St. Lawrence
gathered the sick, orphaned, blind,
and impoverished people the Church
had been supporting. He then
presented what he described as the
"Church's treasure."

Enraged, the prefect ordered him to
be put to death. St. Lawrence was
tied to a grill over a slow fire.

ARROZ CON POLLO
Rice with Chicken

A TRADITIONAL DISH that likely originated in Spain but gained popularity throughout Latin America as well, this rice-chicken entrée resembles in many ways the Spanish classic paella, minus the seafood and other additional ingredients. This robust dish is easy to prepare and can feed a hungry crowd.

1. Sprinkle the chicken pieces with salt and pepper. In a large, deep saucepan, heat the oil over medium heat, and sauté the chicken pieces until golden on all sides. Remove the chicken, place in a covered baking dish, and keep warm in the oven. Add the onion, 6 tablespoons of parsley, and garlic to the saucepan, and cook over medium heat until the onion is soft. Add the broth, wine, roasted red or green peppers, peas, paprika, and saffron. Stir well, and bring the mixture to a boil over medium heat.

2. Add the rice, increase the heat to medium high, and cook, uncovered, for about 20 minutes, stirring occasionally, until the rice is almost tender but some liquid remains. Bury the chicken pieces in the rice. Cover, reduce the heat to low, and cook for about 20 minutes. Turn the rice and the chicken over with a fork from bottom to top. Cover, and cook over low heat for another 10 minutes. Transfer the rice and chicken to a serving platter, and garnish with the remaining parsley.

Use turmeric sparingly as a saffron substitute, since its acrid flavor can easily overwhelm the food.

INGREDIENTS

SERVES 4 TO 6

One 3-pound **chicken**, cut into serving pieces, or 3 pounds skinless, boneless **chicken pieces**

Salt and freshly ground **black pepper** to taste, plus extra as needed

6 tablespoons **extra-virgin olive oil**

1 large **onion**, peeled and chopped

½ cup plus 1 tablespoon **parsley**, chopped

4 tablespoons chopped **garlic**

3½ cups **chicken broth**

½ cup **dry white wine** or **water**

2 roasted **red** or **green peppers**, thinly sliced

½ cup **peas** (optional)

2 tablespoons **smoked paprika**

1 teaspoon **saffron** (see note)

2 cups **long-grain white rice**

SAINTLY MEAL *for* AUGUST

ST. PHILOMENA

A Greek Meal

Piperies me Ntomata Saltsa
Banana Peppers in Tomato Sauce

Kotopoulo Scharas
Greek Marinated Grilled Chicken

Melitzanes Kourkouti
Crispy Eggplant with Tomato Sauce

Halvas Simigdalenios
Semolina Sweets

ST. PHILOMENA

AUGUST 11

Born:	Died:	
291	304	Patron saint of infants, babies, and youth

St. Philomena was the beautiful thirteen-year-old daughter of a Greek prince, born to her parents after they converted to Christianity. She accompanied her parents to a meeting with the Roman emperor Diocletian, who desired her and demanded that she marry him. But St. Philomena, who had vowed her virginity to God, refused. Her response enraged the emperor, who had her imprisoned and tortured. She was scourged; attached to an anchor and dropped into the Tiber River; and shot with numerous arrows. In each situation, angels intervened, saved her life, and healed her wounds. Her courage in protecting her purity caused many who witnessed her sufferings to convert to Christianity. Infuriated, Diocletian had her beheaded.

In 1802, the remains of a girl were found entombed in the Catacombs of Priscilla in Italy. The grave site was marked by three tiles that read, "Peace to you, Philomena," and bore the signs of her martyrdom: an anchor, arrows, and a lance.

In 1833, three people received revelations about St. Philomena's life. Among these was Mother Maria Luisa de Gesù, a Dominican Tertiary and the foundress of the Oblates of Our Lady of Sorrows. Praying before a statue of St. Philomena, Mother Maria experienced a mystical communication with the saint. Later, the nun received a lengthy description of St. Philomena's childhood and subsequent tortures.

In 1805, St. Philomena's relics were brought to the Church of Our Lady of Grace in Mugnano, Italy. After her bones were enshrined in the church, countless well-documented miracles occurred. As a result, popes, bishops, and priests began to honor her. Pope Gregory XVI called her the "wonder worker," and many saints had a strong devotion to her. Dedication to St. Philomena continues to grow today, and her sanctuary is still active in Mugnano.

SHOPPING LIST

BAKING SUPPLIES

All-purpose flour	1 cup
Semolina, coarse	1 cup
Semolina, fine	1 cup
Sugar, granulated	2 ½ cups

CONDIMENTS

Olive oil	2 cups
Vegetable oil	1 cup

DAIRY

Feta cheese, crumbled	3 cups

DRY GOODS

Walnut pieces	½ cup

PRODUCE

Banana peppers	8
Eggplant	1 large
Garlic	2 heads
Lemons	8 to 10
Onions	1 large, 1 small
Parsley	1 bunch
Tomatoes, juicy	7 to 9 large

MEAT

Chicken breasts, boneless, skinless	6 (about 2 pounds)

SPICES

Black pepper	to taste
Cinnamon, ground	to taste
Cinnamon stick	1
Oregano, dried	6 tablespoons plus to taste
Paprika, ground	to taste
Salt	to taste
Whole cloves	1 teaspoon

Piperies me Ntomata Saltsa

Banana Peppers in Tomato Sauce

This is a popular Greek dish that can be served as an appetizer or as a side dish with the entrée.

1. Heat the olive oil in a large skillet over medium heat. Add the pepper halves, and season with salt and pepper. Stir the halves until both sides are golden. Remove the peppers from the skillet with a slotted spoon, and set aside.

2. Add the onion and the garlic (if using) to the skillet. Sauté the mixture for 3 to 5 minutes or until the onions become translucent. Add the puréed tomatoes, and stir to combine. Season with salt and paprika. Reduce the heat to medium low, and cook until most of the liquid is absorbed, about 30 minutes, stirring periodically.

3. Return the peppers to the skillet, and cook for about 5 more minutes. Transfer to a serving dish, and top with feta cheese and parsley. Serve hot with pita bread.

INGREDIENTS

SERVES 4

4 tablespoons **olive oil**

8 **banana peppers**, washed, halved, and seeded

Salt and freshly ground **black pepper** to taste

2 cloves **garlic**, peeled and minced (optional)

1 small **onion**, peeled and chopped

2 or 3 large, juicy **tomatoes**, puréed

Paprika, ground, to taste

Crumbled **feta cheese** for topping (optional)

Parsley, chopped, for topping (optional)

Kotopoulo Scharas

Greek Marinated Grilled Chicken

A classic Greek dish loved for its straightforward preparation and honest flavors, this dish may well have been popular in St. Philomena's time when all the basic ingredients were available. The donor for this version noted that her family increased the amount of olive oil to add more flavor and texture to the dish. Adding chopped fresh herbs could also personalize the recipe. If desired, cube the cooked chicken and use the pieces in a robust salad.

1. Rinse and pat dry the chicken breasts. Place them in a gallon-size plastic bag. Scatter the garlic slices over the front and back of the chicken, and set the bag aside.

2. Mix the lemon juice, olive oil, oregano, and salt together in a medium bowl. Pour the marinade into the bag over the chicken. Carefully remove any excess air from the bag, seal it, and gently squeeze the bag to distribute the marinade. Place the bag in a bowl, and refrigerate it for 6 hours or overnight.

3. Preheat the grill or broiler, and remove the chicken from the refrigerator to bring to room temperature. If grilling, lightly oil the grate. Discard the marinade and grill the breasts, turning once, for 7 to 8 minutes or until their internal temperature reaches 165 degrees. To broil the breasts, place them on a rack midway in the oven, and cook, turning often, until their internal temperature reaches 165 degrees. Remove from the heat, and serve.

INGREDIENTS

SERVES 6

6 boneless, skinless **chicken breasts** (about 2 pounds; for larger breasts, double the marinade quantity)

6 cloves **garlic**, peeled and sliced

1 ½ cups fresh **lemon juice** (about 8 to 10 lemons)

¾ cup **olive oil**

6 tablespoons **oregano**, dried

2 teaspoons **salt**

Melitzanes Kourkouti

Crispy Eggplant with Tomato Sauce

This dish is a variation of an older recipe that is still prepared throughout Greece. Since the eggplant slices are fried in a batter, they have a crispy texture.

1. Preheat the oven to 350 degrees. Line a baking sheet with parchment paper, and set aside.

2. Wash and cut the eggplant lengthwise into ¼-inch-thick slices. Place the slices on a tray, and sprinkle them with salt to extract the bitter juices. Set aside for 15 minutes.

3. Pat the excess water off the eggplant slices with paper towels. Move the slices to a baking sheet, and place it in the oven. Bake them for 5 minutes to dry them. Remove them from the oven, and let them cool completely.

4. Heat 4 tablespoons of olive oil in a medium-size pot over medium heat. Add the onion, and cook until soft, about 5 minutes. Add the garlic, and sauté for 2 to 3 minutes or until golden. Stir in the tomatoes, salt, and pepper, and reduce the heat to low. Cook for about 60 minutes or until the sauce thickens.

5. To make the batter, combine the flour, the spices, and 1 cup of water in a mixing bowl, and whisk until the batter is smooth. Coat the eggplant slices with the batter on both sides.

6. Heat the remaining olive oil in a deep skillet over medium heat for about 1 minute. Add the battered eggplant slices, and fry until the bottom sides are golden. Using two spatulas, carefully turn the slices over to brown the second side. Remove the slices from the skillet, and drain them on paper towels. Brown the remaining eggplant slices, adding more oil as needed.

7. Place the eggplant slices in a baking dish, and pour the tomato sauce over them. Add the crumbled feta, and return to the oven for a few minutes until the feta starts to turn golden. Remove from the oven, and garnish with the chopped parsley. Serve immediately.

INGREDIENTS

SERVES 4

1 large **eggplant**, stem removed

1 cup **olive oil**, or more as needed for frying

1 large **onion**, peeled and chopped

6 **garlic cloves**, peeled and minced

5 or 6 large juicy **tomatoes**, such as beefsteak, puréed

Salt and freshly ground **black pepper** to taste

1 cup **all-purpose flour**

Oregano, dried, to taste

Paprika, ground, to taste

2 cups crumbled **feta cheese** for topping

1 cup fresh **parsley**, chopped

Halvas Simigdalenios

Semolina Sweets

For a fancy presentation, use a pretty 6-cup mold.
Otherwise, use individual serving bowls.

1. To prepare the syrup, combine 4 cups of water and the sugar in a medium-size saucepan, and bring to a boil over medium heat. Keep stirring until the sugar has dissolved. Add the cinnamon stick, lemon peel, and cloves. Continue to cook for about 20 minutes, stirring as needed. Remove from the heat, and strain. Discard the cinnamon stick, lemon peel, and cloves. Set the syrup aside.

2. Heat the oil in a medium-size saucepan over medium heat, and stir in the two semolinas and the walnuts. Reduce the heat to low, and stir often for 10 to 15 minutes. The mixture should turn a golden brown. Remove from the heat.

3. Carefully and slowly pour the syrup over the semolina-and-walnut mix, stirring gently. Take care not to get burned by the bubbling mixture. Transfer the mixture to a 6-cup mold or to individual bowls, and let it cool. To serve, unmold onto a plate, sprinkle with cinnamon, and serve.

INGREDIENTS

SERVES 4

SYRUP

2½ cups **sugar**

1 **cinnamon stick**

1 large piece **lemon peel** without pith

1 teaspoon whole **cloves**

PASTRY

1 cup **vegetable oil**

1 cup **fine semolina**

1 cup **coarse semolina**

½ cup **walnut pieces**

Ground **cinnamon** for sprinkling

A Prayer to

ST. PHILOMENA

O St. Philomena, virgin and martyr, pray for us,
that through your powerful intercession we may
obtain that purity of mind and heart that leads to
the perfect love of God. Amen.

—Website of the St. Philomena
Sanctuary in Mugnano, Italy

AUGUST 14

ST. MAXIMILIAN MARY KOLBE
— Poland —

Born: 1894, Died: 1941

St. Maximilian Kolbe always focused his energies on the Church. As a priest, he traveled throughout Poland to evangelize. He founded a publishing center and a magazine called *Knight of the Immaculate*. He also founded a Franciscan monastery near Warsaw.

After the Nazis invaded Poland, St. Maximilian was sent to the Auschwitz concentration camp. When ten randomly chosen prisoners were sentenced to be starved to death, St. Maximilian volunteered to take the place of a man who had a wife and children. Until their deaths, St. Maximilian led his fellow prisoners in prayers daily. Eventually, the few who survived were given lethal injections. St. Maximilian faced his death calmly and with great courage.

KISZONA KAPUSTA SUPPE
Sauerkraut Soup

SAUERKRAUT IS A POPULAR INGREDIENT in Eastern Europe, and each country has its own name for this fermented shredded cabbage. In Poland, the name is *kapusta*, and this traditional Polish soup recipe was handed down to Deacon Paul Ochenkowski from his grandmother. He explained, "I was blessed by God to have one of my grandparents—my maternal grandmother—live until I was almost forty. I would sit in her kitchen in Connecticut and talk with her about family history and Polish cooking. In the early 1980s, during one of those kitchen visits, I had the presence of mind to get her to tell me her recipe for Kapusta (in original Polish, *kapusniak*) Soup—a favorite on New Year's Day in her house but also good on any cold day as a soup or as a main dish with some hearty bread."

1. Soak the split peas, dried beans, and barley overnight. The next day, heat about 2 tablespoons of olive oil in a large soup pot over medium heat. Add 2 quarts of water, and bring to a boil. Add the soaked beans, and cook for one hour. Check to see if the beans are tender; if not, cook longer until they are.

2. Add the sauerkraut and its juice and the fresh cabbage, and cook for another 30 minutes. Add the butter while the sauerkraut mixture is cooking. Sauté the second onion and the mushrooms in some olive oil until the onions are golden.

3. Add the onion-mushroom mixture to the soup. Cook for another 15 to 20 minutes. Add the 2 tablespoons of dried oatmeal, stir, and turn off the heat. Allow to cook on residual heat for about 5 minutes, and then serve.

Use plain canned sauerkraut, not the type with caraway seeds.

INGREDIENTS
SERVES 4 TO 6

¾ cup dry **split peas**

½ cup dried **beans**, such as Lima, peas, or Great Northern

¼ cup dry **pearl barley**

2 medium **onions**, peeled and chopped

2 to 3 tablespoons **olive oil**, or as needed

One 15- to 16-ounce can **sauerkraut**, undrained (see note)

1 cup shredded fresh **cabbage**

One 8-ounce box fresh **mushrooms**, or more as desired, sliced

½ to ¾ cup **butter** or **margarine**

2 tablespoons dry **oatmeal** to thicken the soup

AUGUST 28

ST. AUGUSTINE OF HIPPO
— *Algeria* —

Born: 354, Died: 430

St. Augustine, the son of St. Monica, who transformed himself from a dissolute pagan to one of Christianity's greatest champions, was an outstanding intellectual. He studied literature and poetry in order to become a public speaker. During this time, he began a philosophical search for the basic truths of life and creation. Later, he was converted and baptized by St. Ambrose.

In 391, St. Augustine was ordained a priest in the city of Hippo and soon became bishop. For the next thirty-five years, he debated with groups who were attacking Christianity and succeeded in preserving the Faith in his community. Church historians credit St. Augustine with having as much influence on Christianity as the authors of the Gospels.

TCHAKCHOUKA

This East Algerian dish has many variations, which include eggs, French fries, and even Algerian sausages. It is a popular summer dish because it can include leftover or extra seasonal vegetables. If you want over-easy eggs, you can fry them in a different pan and then place them on top of the mixture prior to serving with French bread.

Heat a cast-iron skillet over medium-high heat, and cook the onion slices until softened. Add the oil, and sauté the onions for 4 minutes. Add the tomatoes, peppers, zucchini, and garlic, mixing well. Reduce the heat to medium low, and cook, stirring often, for 15 to 20 minutes more. Add the cilantro, paprika, ground chili, and salt and pepper, stirring well. Cook for about 10 minutes more or until its consistency resembles a stew.

INGREDIENTS

SERVES 4

1 **red** or **yellow onion**, peeled and thinly sliced

4 tablespoons **olive oil**

3 **tomatoes**, diced

1 **red bell pepper**, seeded and diced

1 **green bell pepper**, seeded diced

1 **zucchini**, thinly sliced

1 teaspoon **garlic**, minced

Sprigs of **cilantro**, chopped

Paprika, ground, to taste

Chili, ground, to taste

Salt and freshly ground **black pepper** to taste

SEPTEMBER

SEPTEMBER 5

ST. TERESA OF CALCUTTA

— Albania —

Born: 1910, Died: 1997

St. Teresa of Calcutta, familiarly known as Mother Teresa, led a life of saintly devotion to Jesus and the poor, becoming one of the most famous persons of the twentieth century.

In 1929, St. Teresa was sent to Calcutta, India, making her final profession as a nun in 1937. Later, she experienced an interior call from Jesus to devote the rest of her life to the poorest of the poor. She went on to establish the Missionaries of Charity to care for the naked, the hungry, and the poor. Soon she opened the first hospice and refuge for the dying. Patients received medical care and the chance to die with dignity, regardless of their faith.

KURABIE
Albanian Lemon Butter Cookies

MAKES 100 COOKIES

USUALLY THE COOKIES ARE EATEN AS IS because they remain tender and flaky for days at a time. But many Albanians—and probably others—turn them into a simple dessert by soaking them in sugar water. For a much stronger lemon punch, add 1 tablespoon of lemon zest.

1. Preheat the oven to 350 degrees. Line 2 or 3 baking sheets with parchment paper, and set aside.

2. Mix together the flour, yogurt, granulated sugar, butter, eggs, baking soda, and lemon zest in a large mixing bowl. When the dough becomes flaky, turn it onto a clean surface. Butter your hands with the melted butter to knead the dough and shape it into small walnut shapes. Place the cookies on the baking sheets, spacing them 1 inch apart. Brush them with the beaten egg yolks.

3. Bake for 20 minutes or until firm. Remove the cookies from the oven, cool, and dust with confectioners' sugar.

INGREDIENTS

4 cups **all-purpose flour**

1 cup **plain yogurt**, preferably Greek

1 cup **granulated sugar**

½ cup (4 ounces) **unsalted butter**, softened

3 large **eggs**

1 teaspoon **baking soda**

1 teaspoon **lemon zest**, or more to taste

2 tablespoons melted **butter**, to rub on hands

1 or 2 beaten **egg yolks**, to brush

Confectioners' sugar, to dust

SAINTLY MEAL
for
SEPTEMBER

ST. PETER CLAVER

A Colombian Menu

Arroz con Coco
Rice with Coconut Milk

Cartagena-Style Seafood with Coconut Milk

Enyucado
Yucca Cake

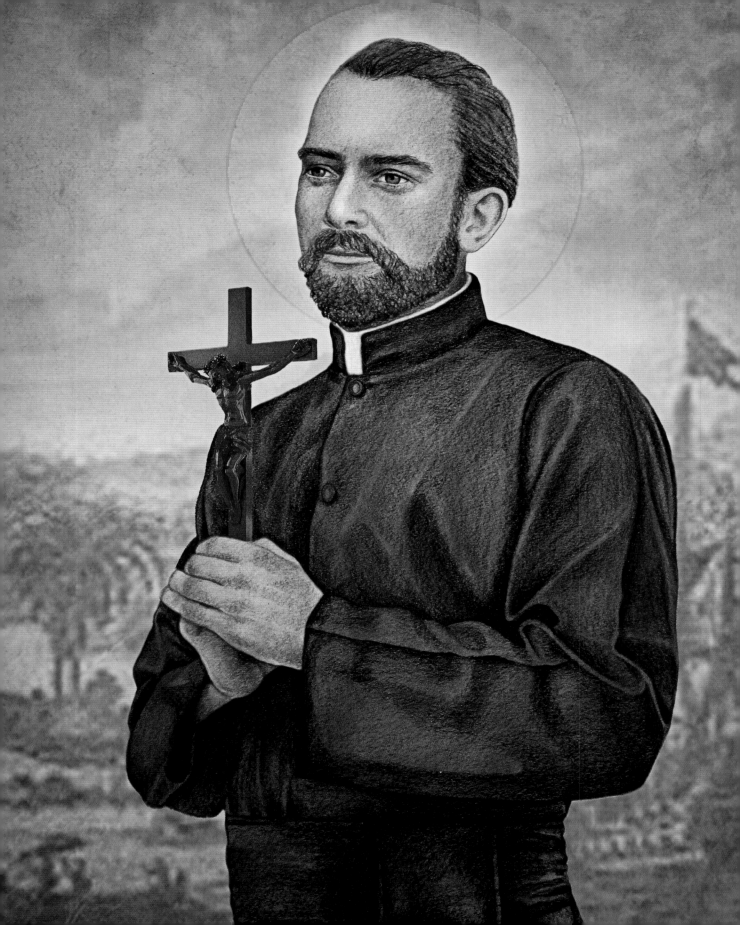

ST. PETER CLAVER

SEPTEMBER 9

Born:	Died:	Patron saint of slaves, race relations, ministry to African Americans, seafarers, and Colombia
1581	1654	

Born Pedro Claver y Corberó in Catalonia, Spain, into a pious Catholic family, St. Peter attended the University of Barcelona. Upon graduation at the age of twenty, he entered the Society of Jesus. Before being ordained a priest, St. Peter volunteered to serve in Cartagena, Colombia, where he witnessed the cruel treatment of African slaves shipped into the country to work in the mines.

St. Peter decided to devote his life to ministering to the slaves, who were often neglected and suffered from many diseases. St. Peter would visit them on the incoming ships or go to the holding areas, taking them food and medicine. When not tending to incoming slave ships, he visited villages or farms where slaves worked, preaching the Word of God. In his forty years of ministry, St. Peter baptized about three hundred thousand slaves. In addition,

he tended to the spiritual needs of the upper classes, resident Muslims, and Protestants.

In the last few years of his life, St. Peter's health declined dramatically, and he suffered so much that he could not leave his residence. When the people of Cartagena learned of his death, many came to pay him respect; he had forged an outstanding reputation as a kindly and saintly priest.

St. Peter's legacy today is extensive: schools, hospitals, and religious groups bear his name, and his works are honored by the Apostles of the Sea and by the Missionary Sisters of St. Peter Claver. A shrine exists in Cartagena called the Church of St. Peter Claver.

St. Peter Claver was beatified in 1851 by Pope Pius IX and was canonized in 1888 by Pope Leo XIII.

SHOPPING LIST

BAKING SUPPLIES

Sugar, granulated — 1 ½ cups or more to taste

CANNED GOODS

Coconut milk — two 14-ounce cans

CONDIMENTS

Coconut oil — 3 tablespoons

Olive oil — 6 tablespoons

Soy sauce — ½ teaspoon

Thai fish sauce — ½ teaspoon

DAIRY

Butter, unsalted — 1 tablespoon

Heavy cream — 2 tablespoons

Queso fresco, grated — 1 ½ cups

DRY GOODS

Raisins — ¾ cup

Rice, jasmine — 4 cups

PRODUCE

Coconut, grated — 1 cup

Garlic — 2 cloves

Green or yellow bell pepper — 1

Onion, red — ½

Red bell pepper — 1

Tomato — 1 large

Yucca, grated — 3 cups

SEAFOOD

Mahi-mahi, grouper, or **salmon** — 1 pound

Shrimp — 1 pound

SPICES

Anise seeds — 1 tablespoon

Black pepper — to taste

Curry powder — ½ teaspoon

Salt — to taste

Seasoned Salt (Lawry's) — 1 teaspoon

Colombian Recipes

As diverse as Colombia is—from the seaside to the plains, to the Amazon region and to mountaintop cities and villages—so too is the cuisine of this country. Cultural influences came from Europe, the Middle East, and Africa. The Colombians have shaped a unique culinary scene that reflects this diversity. Visitors can enjoy tropical fruits, world-renowned coffee, freshly caught Pacific Ocean seafood, and the big-city fare of street vendors and pricey restaurants. The following dishes reflect the table fare of the cities of Barranquilla and Cartagena, where coconut adds the magic touch to drinks, main dishes, and desserts. Some of these recipes can be transformed from daily meals to elegant dinner parties. For example, the coconut rice without the browning step can become a daily white rice cooked in coconut milk. The sauce for the fish can be used with chicken or pork and is equally delicious over mussels, clams, or scallops.

Arroz con Coco

Rice with Coconut Milk

Using the sweet Thai jasmine rice and thick coconut milk yields a golden rich rice dish sparked with the addition of raisins. The initial cooking of the coconut oil over high heat will produce the dark browned oil specks that will cover the final dish and will give it the desired golden color. It is a perfect side dish with pork, fish, and other assorted meats.

1. Heat the 3 tablespoons of coconut oil in a heavy saucepan over medium heat. Add the coconut milk. Cook, stirring occasionally, until the coconut milk starts to darken and form dark edges on the sides of the saucepan. Keep stirring to spread the color. In about twenty minutes, the coconut milk cooks down, separating into oil and lightly browned coconut solids. The coconut oil lightly fries the coconut solids, creating a sweet, toasted coconut mass and highly flavored coconut oil. Once there's a clear separation of oil and solids, add the rice, stirring briskly, to coat all the grains in the hot oil. Add 6 cups of water, the raisins, and the salt, and let it boil until most of the water has evaporated. Reduce the heat to medium low, and cover the saucepan. Simmer until the moisture is absorbed, about 25 to 30 minutes, or until the rice becomes tender.

2. Sprinkle the top with sugar, and then stir it in with a fork. Remove from the heat when the rice is completely tender, and serve hot.

INGREDIENTS

SERVES 8 TO 10

3 tablespoons **coconut oil**

One 14-ounce can **coconut milk**

4 cups **jasmine rice**

1½ teaspoons **salt,** or to taste

¾ cup **raisins**

½ cup **sugar,** or more to taste

Always stir uncooked rice with a wooden spoon, and when cooked, fluff with a fork.

Cartagena-Style Seafood with Coconut Milk

1. Heat 2 tablespoons of oil in a large skillet over medium heat, and sauté the garlic until golden. Remove the garlic and set aside. Add 2 more tablespoons of oil, and sauté the mahi-mahi over medium heat until both sides are golden. Set aside. Repeat with the shrimp, cooking for about 2 to 3 minutes or until the shrimp turn pink. Put the seafood in separate heatproof dishes, and keep them warm in the oven.

2. Pour the remaining oil into the skillet, and add the vegetables and seasonings. Cook over medium heat, stirring often, adding more oil if needed, until the vegetables soften. Stir in the coconut milk, and continue cooking until all the ingredients are incorporated, 2 to 3 minutes.

3. Place the seafood on two serving dishes, and spoon equal amounts of the cooked vegetables over the top. Serve while hot.

 Thai fish sauce can be easily found in the Asian food section of most grocery stores.

INGREDIENTS

SERVES 6 TO 8

6 tablespoons **olive oil**

1 teaspoon **garlic**, minced

1 pound **mahi-mahi fillets** or a fish of solid consistency, such as **grouper** or **salmon**

1 pound peeled and deveined **shrimp**

1 **red pepper**, seeded and cut into strips

1 **green** or **yellow pepper**, seeded and cut into strips

1 large **tomato**, cut into strips

½ **red onion**, peeled and thinly sliced

1 teaspoon **Seasoned Salt** (Lawry's)

½ teaspoon **Thai fish sauce** (see note)

½ teaspoon **soy sauce**

½ teaspoon **curry powder**

½ teaspoon **salt**

¼ teaspoon ground **black pepper**

1 ½ cups **coconut milk**

Enyucado

Yucca Cake

Enyucado, roughly translated "Yucca Cake," is a popular Colombian dessert composed of shredded coconut, coconut milk, and shredded yucca (*yuca* in Spanish and also known as *cassava*). This dessert comes from the Caribbean area of the country but is enjoyed everywhere. Some cooks roast or fry the mixture, but this version calls for baking it. Queso fresco is sold at international and Latin markets. An alternative is to use a Colombian-style white farmer's cheese called queso costeño, also sold at international and Latin markets.

1. Preheat the oven to 400 degrees. Spray a 9 x 13-inch baking dish with cooking spray, and set aside.

2. In a large bowl, combine the yucca, grated coconut, coconut milk, and butter. Stir until the mixture is well combined. Stir in the cheese, sugar, heavy cream, anise, and salt. Spread evenly in the baking dish.

3. Bake for 45 to 50 minutes, or until the center is firm and the top has turned golden. Remove from the oven, allow to cool for 10 to 15 minutes, and then cut into squares or diamonds. Eat hot or at room temperature.

SERVES 10 TO 12

3 cups grated **yucca**

1 cup grated **coconut**

1 cup **coconut milk**

1 tablespoon **unsalted butter**, softened

1½ cups grated **queso fresco**

1 cup **sugar**

2 tablespoons **heavy cream**

1 tablespoon **anise seeds**

Pinch **salt**

Prayer to

ST. PETER CLAVER

O God, who made Saint Peter Claver a slave
of slaves and strengthened him with wonderful
charity and patience as he came to their help,
grant, through his intercession, that, seeking
the things of Jesus Christ, we may love our
neighbor in deeds and in truth. Through
our Lord Jesus Christ, Your Son, who lives
and reigns with You in the unity of the Holy
Spirit, one God, for ever and ever. Amen.

—From the U.S. Proper of Saints in the *Roman Missal*

SEPTEMBER 20

ST. ANDREW KIM TAEGON

— *Korea* —

Born: 1821, Died: 1846

St. Andrew Kim Taegon (also known as Andreas Kim Tae-Gon and Andeurea Gim Dae-Geon), was the first Korean-born Catholic priest. The son of converts—his father was martyred in 1839—St. Andrew was baptized at the age of fifteen. He went to Macau, an autonomous territory on the southern border of China, to attend seminary. While in seminary, he returned often to Korea to work in missions. After he finished seminary, he was ordained a priest in Shanghai in 1844. He returned to Korea to preach and evangelize despite the ongoing persecution of Christians. After only two years, St. Andrew was arrested, tortured, and beheaded near the capital city of Seoul at the young age of twenty-five.

MANDOO
Korean Dumplings
MAKES ABOUT 40 DUMPLINGS

Mandoo, or Korean dumplings, are minced meat and vegetables wrapped in a thin sheet of dough. The most popular fillings are ground beef or pork, shrimp, bean sprouts, scallions, and shredded kimchi. Cooking options include boiling, steaming, deep- or pan-frying, or cooking in a soup or stew. The word *mandoo* may also be spelled *mandu*. Korean chives are sold in Asian markets, but an acceptable substitute is the green stems of scallions. Mandoo, or dumpling, wrappers are sold at Asian markets, well-stocked supermarkets, and online. Select the larger ones, if possible.

1. Mince the shrimp, and set aside. Using a cheesecloth, strain out any remaining water from the tofu. In separate containers, sprinkle the chopped cabbage, the diced zucchini, and the diced onion with salt. Set aside for 30 minutes, then strain out any remaining water.

2. In a large bowl, stir the tofu, cabbage, zucchini, and onions into the scallions and chives. Add the garlic, salt, pepper, sesame seeds, sake (if using), and sesame oil, and stir well.

3. Divide the mixed ingredients into two bowls. Mix half with beef and pork, and half into the bowl with shrimp. Stir well. Put about 1 tablespoon of the above mixture in the center of a dumpling wrapper, adjusting the amount as desired. Then seal the edges together by lightly wetting them with water or beaten egg and pressing the edges together.

4. Steam or boil the prepared dumplings. To steam them, line the steamer with a paper towel or cheesecloth. Then steam the dumplings for about 20 minutes. To boil them, bring water to a boil in a pot; then add the dumplings. Stir once or twice gently until the water boils again. When the dumplings float to the top, add ½ cup of cold water. When the water boils again, remove and strain the dumplings and rinse them under cold water.

INGREDIENTS

1 pound fresh **shrimp**, rinsed in salt water, peeled, and deveined

3 pounds **firm tofu**, crumbled

½ head **Napa cabbage**, chopped

1 **zucchini**, diced

1 pound **onions**, peeled and diced

1 bunch **scallions**, chopped

1 bunch **Korean chives**, chopped

4 cloves **garlic**, minced

1 teaspoon **salt**

1 teaspoon **pepper**, ground

1 tablespoon **sesame seeds**

1 tablespoon **sesame oil**

½ pound **ground beef**

½ pound **ground pork**

2 packages mandoo **dumpling wrappers**

1 teaspoon **sake** (optional)

SEPTEMBER 23

ST. PADRE PIO

— *Italy* —

Born: 1887, Died: 1968

Despite persistent illness, St. Pio entered the Capuchin novitiate at age fifteen. When his stigmata appeared, he bore the piercings to his feet, hands, and side with composure and resignation. The wounds oozed blood but never became infected, and they emitted the fragrance of roses. Letters to his spiritual counselors reveal his tremendous suffering, both physical and spiritual.

As word of his ministry spread, pilgrims came to St. Pio for confessions and spiritual guidance. Because of his renown, more than one hundred thousand people attended his funeral. His body remains incorrupt.

Padre Pio is undoubtedly one of the most remarkable Catholic saints: performing miracles, bilocating, and levitating. His other gifts included healing, discernment of spirits, and prophecy.

ROSE PETAL COOKIES

MAKES ABOUT 3½ DOZEN 2-INCH COOKIES

ST. PADRE PIO WAS THE SOURCE OF MANY MIRACULOUS EVENTS, but perhaps the least well known is this: according to historians and to witnesses, he often emitted a strong rose fragrance, even when he was not nearby and even after his demise. Organic food-grade dried rose petals are readily available online. Some well-stocked supermarkets and specialty food stores carry rose essence.

1. Place the butter and sugar in a bowl, and using an electric mixer, beat them together until light and creamy. Add the vanilla extract, rose essence, and salt, and mix until blended. Add the flour, and combine at low speed until just mixed. When the dough becomes sticky, gently fold in the rose petals by hand. Shape the dough into a ball, wrap it in foil, and refrigerate for at least 2 hours or overnight.

2. Preheat the oven to 325 degrees. Line 2 or 3 baking sheets with parchment paper. On a lightly floured surface, roll the dough out to a thickness of ¼ inch, and use a 2-inch round cookie cutter to cut out the cookies. Place the cookies on the baking sheets about ½ inch apart.

3. Bake for 8 to 10 minutes, or until the cookies begin to turn golden brown on the underside. Cool completely before dusting with confectioners' sugar, if desired.

INGREDIENTS

1 cup (8 ounces) **unsalted butter**, at room temperature

½ cup plus 2 tablespoons **sugar**

1 teaspoon **vanilla extract**

½ to 1 teaspoon **rose essence**

½ teaspoon **salt**

2 cups **all-purpose flour**, or more as needed

3 tablespoons **dried rose petals**

Confectioners' sugar for dusting (optional)

SEPTEMBER 27

ST. VINCENT DE PAUL

— France —

Born: 1581, Died: 1660

Born in Gascony, France, St. Vincent de Paul is one of the most memorable Catholic saints, with societies, charities, schools, thrift shops, and churches bearing his name today.

St. Vincent felt inspired to spend his life helping the poor, both materially and spiritually. After becoming the parish priest of Clichy, he devoted himself entirely to forming missions and giving aid to the poor. He founded hospitals and started an association of wealthy laywomen who cared for the sick and the poor.

St. Vincent is known as "the Apostle of Charity." His incorrupt heart is held today at the Convent of the Daughters of Charity in Paris.

GALETTES DE POMMES DE TERRE
Potato Cakes

MAKES 12 TO 15 PATTIES

THESE CAKES TAKE A LITTLE EFFORT TO MAKE because the dough needs rolling and chilling. Serve as an appetizer or a side dish. Note: You can modify this recipe by adding diced ham or mushrooms when adding the goat cheese. For very smooth potatoes, use an immersion blender.

1. Boil the potatoes until fork tender, and drain. Mash the potatoes until smooth, and set aside until cold.

2. Blend the butter with the cheese, chives, rosemary, and garlic, and shape it into a flat block, about 4 inches by 6 inches. Chill for 15 minutes.

3. Mix about 1½ cups of flour, or more as needed, into the potatoes to form a soft dough. Flour a work surface, and roll the dough out into a ¼-inch-thick rectangle, about 9 inches by 16 inches. Place the cheese block in the center, and fold up the dough along the long sides of the cheese block to cover the cheese. Fold over the bottom third, and fold over the top third to cover the first layer of dough. Crimp the edges with a fork.

4. Cover the pastry, and chill for 15 minutes. Then repeat the rolling and folding twice more, and chill between each folding. Chill the last time for one hour.

5. Preheat the oven to 375 degrees. Line a baking sheet with parchment paper, and set aside.

6. Roll out the dough, cut it into 12 to 15 pieces, and shape them into patties. Place them on the baking sheet, and brush the tops with the egg wash.

7. Bake for 15 minutes, remove from the oven, and brush with the egg wash again. Bake for another 15 minutes until the underside of the patties is golden brown. Remove from the oven, turn the patties over, brush with the egg wash, and bake for 5 more minutes. Serve warm.

INGREDIENTS

2 large (1½ pounds) **russet potatoes**, peeled and diced

1½ to 2 cups **all-purpose flour** plus extra for rolling dough

4 tablespoons (½ stick) **unsalted butter**, at room temperature

4 ounces fresh **goat cheese**

3 tablespoons **chives**, minced

2 tablespoons **rosemary**, chopped

1 tablespoon **garlic**, minced

1 **egg yolk** mixed with 1 tablespoon **water**, for glazing

Salt and freshly ground **black pepper** to taste

OCTOBER

OCTOBER 1

ST. THÉRÈSE OF LISIEUX

— France —

Born: 1873, Died: 1897

St. Thérèse of Lisieux felt an intense calling to the contemplative life. At age fifteen, she entered a Carmelite convent. There she practiced her "Little Way," doing the little things of daily life with great love. Living as she did in humility, simplicity, and solitude, she had an intimate connection to God.

In her autobiography, *Story of a Soul*, St. Thérèse describes herself as the "little flower of Jesus," glorifying God among all the other flowers in His garden. After her death, she said, she would send a shower of roses to earth to encourage people to love God.

St. Thérèse suffered from tuberculosis and died at the age of twenty-four, leaving behind a monumental legacy.

HIMMLISCHE ROSENBLÜTEN TORTE
Heavenly Rose Petal Torte

SERVES 10 TO 12

CARMELITE NUN ST. THÉRÈSE OF LISIEUX, whom Pope Pius X named the "greatest saint of modern times," promised that in heaven she would "let fall a shower of roses." Enjoying rose-based recipes is a good way to honor her. Rose petal jam and rose petals are available online. The cream filling and topping may be prepared a day ahead. Save the egg whites for the recipe the next day. The following recipe is separated into three parts: the cake, the filling and topping, and the decoration.

FOR THE CAKE

1. Preheat the oven to 350 degrees. Line the bottom of an 8-inch springform pan with parchment paper. Before pouring the batter into the pan, spray the edges with vegetable spray. Set aside.

2. Using an electric mixer, beat the sugar and butter until creamy. Add the rose essence and vanilla extract.

3. In a separate large bowl combine the egg whites with the warm water and lemon juice, and stir by hand. Using an electric mixer, beat them until a soft peak forms.

4. Mix together the flour, baking powder, baking soda, finely ground almonds, and salt. Fold the dry ingredients by hand into the egg white mixture in several small batches. Then, also by hand, fold in the butter mixture and the dried rose petals. Pour the batter into the prepared springform pan.

5. Bake for 45 minutes or until a cake tester inserted in the center comes out clean. Transfer to a cooling rack. Remove the outer ring after 15 minutes. When the cake is completely cool, transfer it to a serving plate. With a large knife cut the cake into 2 layers. Carefully transfer the top layer to another plate, and turn it upside down.

CAKE INGREDIENTS

1 cup **sugar**

½ cup (4 ounces) **unsalted butter**, at room temperature

2 teaspoons **rose essence**

1 teaspoon **vanilla extract**

1½ cups **cake flour**, sifted

1 teaspoon **baking powder**

1 teaspoon **baking soda**

½ cup **almonds**, peeled and finely ground

¼ teaspoon **salt**

1 cup dried food-grade **rose petals**

8 **egg whites**, at room temperature

⅓ cup **warm water**

1 tablespoon plus 1 teaspoon **lemon juice**

FOR THE CREAM FILLING AND TOPPING

1. Prepare the cream filling and topping by beating together the egg yolks with the sugar, cornstarch, vanilla extract, and salt until smooth.

2. Heat the milk, stirring often, over medium-low heat; bring to a boil. As soon as it boils, remove it from the heat. Stirring constantly with a whisk, pour half the hot milk into the egg yolk mixture to warm it and to prevent curdling. Transfer the egg mixture to the saucepan with the remaining milk, and stirring constantly with the whisk, heat again over medium-high heat. The mixture will thicken quickly. After it comes to a boil, stir 1 more minute. Remove from the heat, and whisk in the butter.

3. Transfer the cream to a bowl, cover it with plastic wrap so the wrap touches the surface to prevent a skin from forming, and refrigerate for at least 2 hours or overnight.

FOR THE DECORATION

To prepare for serving, spoon or brush an even coat of rose petal jam on top and around the sides of the bottom layer. Reserve 1 cup of the cream filling, and set aside. Spread the remaining filling on top of the rose petal jam. Spread an even coat of rose petal jam on the underside of the top layer. Gently turn the top layer right side up, and place it gingerly on top of the prepared layer. Repeat, applying the rose petal jam to the sides of the top layer. Use the remaining cream filling to coat the top of the tart evenly. Dust the top with a very fine coat of cocoa. Cover with the stencil (if using), and follow with a dusting of confectioners' sugar. Remove the stencil. Place the fresh rose petals all around the edge of the cake to stick to the jam. Refrigerate until ready to use, or serve immediately.

CREAM FILLING AND TOPPING INGREDIENTS

8 **egg yolks**, at room temperature

4 tablespoons **sugar**

3 tablespoons **cornstarch**

1 tablespoon **vanilla extract**

Pinch **salt**

2 cups **whole milk**

2 tablespoons **unsalted butter**, softened

DECORATION INGREDIENTS

One 9 ½-ounce jar **rose petal jam**

Extra-fine **cocoa powder** for dusting

Rose-theme stencil (optional)

Confectioners' sugar, for dusting

Organically grown **rose petals**

OCTOBER 5

ST. MARIA FAUSTINA KOWALSKA

— Poland —

Born: 1905, Died: 1938

At age nineteen, St. Maria Faustina had a vision of Jesus, inspiring her to go to a local cathedral, where she received the message that she must travel to Warsaw to find a convent. In Warsaw, she joined the Congregation of the Sisters of Our Lady of Mercy.

Later, St. Faustina received a series of visits from Jesus. He tasked her with spreading devotion to His most merciful heart, showing her an image of Himself with rays of light emanating from His heart. The image was painted, and the inscription "Jesus, I trust in You" was added beneath it.

After St. Faustina's death, the devotion to Divine Mercy spread worldwide.

KREMÓWKA PAPIESKA
Papal Cream Cake

THIS CAKE EARNED ITS PAPAL NAME when Pope St. John Paul II commented during a 1999 visit to his former hometown of Wadowice, Poland, that he loved the traditional cream cake he used to enjoy as a child. He was quite surprised when, the next day, numerous town residents appeared with portions of this cake—hence, the name Papal Cream Cake.

The cake's popularity is enduring, even after so many decades. It was presented by Poland as their contribution to the European Union's fiftieth birthday party.

1. Preheat the oven to 400 degrees. Line a baking pan with parchment paper. Unfold each sheet of puff pastry on the baking pan, and score each sheet with a knife into 9 or more even sections. Do not cut all the way through the dough. Cover each sheet with parchment paper, and place a wire cooling rack or a baking sheet on top. This will keep the pastry flat and allow it to bake.

2. Bake for 15 minutes, remove from the oven, and let cool completely.

3. Meanwhile, to make the pastry cream, start by dissolving the cornstarch in 2 cups of cold milk, and set aside. In a medium saucepan, heat the remaining milk, sugar, vanilla extract, and salt over medium-low heat, and bring to a boil, stirring often. Add the milk with the dissolved cornstarch by pouring it through a fine-mesh sieve to avoid adding lumps. Return to a boil, stirring constantly with a wire whisk. Add the egg yolks, and continue stirring constantly. Reduce the heat to low, and continue to cook for 1 minute, stirring constantly. Remove from the heat, and set the saucepan in an ice-water bath to stop the cooking. Do not chill the cream because it will be poured hot over the puff pastry.

INGREDIENTS
SERVES 9 OR MORE

CAKE

One 17-ounce package frozen **puff pastry**, thawed

PASTRY CREAM

½ cup **cornstarch**

4 cups **whole milk**

1½ cups granulated **sugar**

2 teaspoons **vanilla extract**

¼ teaspoon **salt**

12 large **egg yolks**, beaten

Confectioners' sugar, for sprinkling

4. To assemble the cake, use a dish or pan the size of the puff pastry sheets as a mold. Place one layer of the puff pastry in the bottom of the pan. Pour the hot cream over the top, and place the second layer of puff pastry over the filling. Refrigerate the cake until the filling is set.

5. When ready to serve, using the prescored marks as guides, cut into 9 or more pieces. Dust each piece with confectioners' sugar. Refrigerate the leftovers.

Jesus, I trust in You!…*Spes contra spem!* [Hope against hope!] With God nothing is impossible!

What is especially possible is conversion, which can change hatred into love and war into peace.

And so our prayer becomes all the more insistent and trusting: Jesus, I trust in You!

OCTOBER 15

ST. TERESA
OF ÁVILA

— *Spain* —

Born: 1515, Died: 1582

❧

In 1535, St. Teresa joined a Carmelite convent in Ávila, Spain, and took the habit. A year later, illness forced her to return home. While recovering, she read a life-changing book, *Third Spiritual Alphabet* by Fr. Francis de Osuna. The book was about prayers of recollection, and it inspired her to devote herself to prayer and to seeking perfect union with God through contemplation.

Later, St. Teresa returned to the convent, and during the ensuing years, she worked to reform the Carmelites. She wrote for the order a new constitution that called for absolute poverty, and she founded convents of Discalced Carmelite nuns throughout Spain. She spent much time writing books on mystical theology.

PAN DE SANTA TERESA
St. Teresa's Bread

THIS DISH MAKES A TASTY BREAKFAST OR BRUNCH, especially for children. It is a first cousin to French toast, but with a flavor and texture all its own. The milk can be prepared the night before cooking.

1. Combine the milk with the sugar, cinnamon stick, and lemon peel in a saucepan. Heat over medium-low heat, and cook for 5 to 10 minutes or until the milk is well flavored.

2. Place the bread in a large, flat baking pan, and strain the milk over it. Beat the eggs in a shallow bowl with a pinch of salt. With a spatula, lay the slices of bread in the eggs, turning them to coat both sides. Beat additional eggs and salt together to finish coating the bread slices, if necessary. Heat the oil in a large skillet, and fry each slice until browned and crusty on each side. Place on individual plates or a serving dish, and sprinkle with the cinnamon sugar before serving.

INGREDIENTS

SERVES 4 TO 6

2 cups **whole milk**

3 tablespoons **sugar**

1 **cinnamon stick**

1 **lemon peel**, sliced

12 slices 2-day-old **Italian** or **French bread**, sliced ½ to ¾ inch thick

3 large **eggs**

Pinch **salt**

3 to 4 tablespoons **olive oil**, for frying, or more as needed

Cinnamon sugar for sprinkling

OCTOBER 21

ST. LAURA OF ST. CATHERINE OF SIENA

— Colombia —

Born: 1874, Died: 1949

St. Laura's family was extremely poor, especially following her father's death during the Colombian Civil War. To help her impoverished mother, St. Laura studied to become a teacher and taught for several years. Experiencing great spiritual growth, she felt drawn to the religious life as a Discalced Carmelite. Even more, she desired to live as a missionary to the native population of South America.

St. Laura, with several other young women, formed the Congregation of Missionary Sisters of the Immaculate Virgin Mary and St. Catherine of Siena. The Sisters lived among the natives and taught them about Jesus Christ. Today the Missionary Sisters work in nineteen countries throughout the Americas, Africa, and Europe.

POLLO GUISADO Y ABORRAJADOS
Chicken Stew and Colombian Fried Plantains

NOT AN EXCLUSIVELY COLOMBIAN DISH, this chicken stew has many versions in other Caribbean and South American homes. Its main ingredients are chicken thighs combined with potatoes, carrots, red peppers, and green beans—a homey comfort meal. Serve as is or over plain rice. A perfect side dish is fried, stuffed plantains (see the recipe on the next page).

FOR THE CHICKEN STEW

1. Heat a large skillet over medium heat. Add the olive oil. When hot, add the onions and garlic. Sauté for 5 to 8 minutes or until the onions are translucent. Add the chicken pieces. Panfry, turning, until all sides have changed color and no more pink is visible, about 5 minutes. Remove from the heat, and set aside.

2. Pour the chicken broth into a large stockpot. Stir in the bay leaves, oregano, adobo powder, and cumin. Add the potatoes and the carrots. Cook for 15 minutes. Add the chicken, onions garlic, green beans, red pepper, diced tomatoes, and tomato cooking base. Cook for another 15 minutes. Adjust seasonings to taste. Remove the bay leaves. Garnish with the chopped cilantro.

3. Alternatively: Combine the chicken broth, plus all the cut-up vegetables, spices, and the sautéed chicken with the onion and garlic in a pressure cooker, and cook on high for 10 minutes. Let it cool naturally for at least 10 minutes, and then release the steam. Mix well, and remove the bay leaves. Garnish with the chopped cilantro, and serve.

Cilantro *is the Spanish word for* coriander. *It is the common term in North American English for coriander leaves, due to their extensive use in Mexican cuisine .*

INGREDIENTS

SERVES 6

⅛ cup **olive oil**

1 large **sweet onion**, peeled and diced

6 **garlic cloves**, peeled and minced

6 **chicken thighs**, sliced in half

4 cups **chicken broth**, homemade or canned

6 to 8 **bay leaves**

2 tablespoons **oregano**, dried

2 teaspoons **Goya brand adobo powder**, or to taste

1 teaspoon ground **cumin**

3 large **potatoes**, cut into 1-inch cubes

2 extra-large **carrots**, cut into ¼-inch slices

2 cups diced **green beans**, or another green vegetable, such as **zucchini**

1 **red pepper**, seeded and chopped

One 14.5-ounce can diced **tomatoes** with juice

½ cup **Sofrito tomato cooking base** or 5 ounces regular **tomato paste**

1 small bunch **cilantro**, rinsed and chopped (see note)

Salt and freshly ground **black pepper** to taste

FOR THE FRIED PLANTAINS

Plantains are staple crops in many countries in Africa, Latin America, and the Caribbean. These are the larger, less-sweet version of the banana. Available in green, mottled black and yellow, and almost black at their ripest, plantains are usually considered a vegetable. Home cooks boil, steam, bake, or fry them, or add them to other dishes, such as soups and stews. When all black, the plantain is at its sweetest and may be used as a dessert.

1.   Slice the ends off the plantains, and then slice through the peel lengthwise several times to help remove the peel. Slice the plantains crosswise into 1½-inch-thick pieces.

2.   Heat several inches of oil in a deep skillet over medium heat to 360 degrees. Fry the plantain slices until golden brown, about 4 minutes. Drain the plantain pieces on paper towels. When cool enough to handle, place each slice between two pieces of wax paper, and use the flat bottom of a glass to flatten the plantain to about ¼-inch thickness.

3.   Sandwich 1 to 2 tablespoons of grated cheese between 2 slices of plantain, pressing the slices together around the edges to seal in the cheese. Repeat with the remaining plantain slices.

4.   Whisk the flour, sugar, baking soda, and salt together. Stir in the eggs and add enough milk to make a thick batter. Stir until well mixed.

5.   Dip the plantain "sandwiches" into the batter to coat them. Then return them to the oil to fry in batches until golden. Drain on paper towels.

INGREDIENTS

SERVES 10

2 **black-and-yellow plantains**

Vegetable oil for deep-frying

½ cup **grated cheese**, such as farmer's cheese, Monterey Jack, or mozzarella

4 tablespoons **all-purpose flour**

2 tablespoons **sugar**

½ teaspoon **baking soda**

½ teaspoon **salt**

2 **eggs**, lightly beaten

1 to 2 tablespoons **whole milk**

SAINTLY MEAL *for* OCTOBER

ST. FRUMENTIUS

An Ethiopian Meal

Yebeg Alicha
Mild Lamb Stew

Messer Wot
Spiced Lentils

Ye'abesha Gomen Wat
Ethiopian Collard Greens

Lab
Ethiopian Cottage Cheese and Yogurt Dessert

ST. FRUMENTIUS

OCTOBER 27

Born:	Died:	Patron saint of the
early 4th century	circa 383	Kingdom of Axum (Aksum), Abyssinia, and Ethiopia

A native of Lebanon, St. Frumentius and his brother Aedesius sailed with their uncle to Ethiopia. Versions of the story differ, one stating that while sailing on the Red Sea, they were shipwrecked, and all the crew except the two boys died. Another version states that while docking at a harbor in the Red Sea, locals attacked the ship and killed all the crew except St. Frumentius and his brother.

The young boys were taken as slaves to the king of Axum (also spelled Aksum; part of Northern Ethiopia), who had them serve him at court. It is recorded that St. Frumentius eventually served as his secretary and even converted the king to Christianity. After the king's death, St. Frumentius was kept on at court at the behest of the queen, who had him educate the young prince. He was also permitted to spread Christianity by preaching to local merchants and to the public at large.

St. Frumentius traveled to Alexandria to ask St. Athanasius, then its patriarch, to send priests and bishops to Ethiopia to help spread Christianity. In response, Athanasius named Frumentius bishop of Ethiopia. Upon his return, St. Frumentius established the founding church in the capital city and, thereafter, many churches throughout the country. Ten years later, Ethiopia became officially a Christian country. Ethiopians named St. Frumentius *Abuna*, "the father of Ethiopia," and *Abba Salama*, "the father of peace."

SHOPPING LIST

BREAD

Injera	8 to 10, 1 for serving plus at least 1 per person
Flat bread	depends on size, enough for all persons

CONDIMENTS

Canola or **vegetable oil**	1 ½ cups
Olive oil (optional)	½ cup

DAIRY

Cottage cheese, small curd or farmer's cheese	1 pound
Ethiopian butter (*niter kibbeh*), or **clarified butter with spice mix**	¼ cup
Yogurt, plain	4 tablespoons

DRY GOODS

Lentils, red, split	2 cups

PRODUCE

Collard greens	2 pounds
Garlic	4 heads

Jalapeño peppers	5 large
Lemon	1
Mixed fruit persons	enough for all
Onion, red	1 large
Onion, red or yellow	1
Onion, yellow	4 large
Parsley	1 bunch

MEAT

Leg of lamb, boneless	2 pounds

SPICES

Berbere	2 to 3 tablespoons
Black pepper	to taste
Cardamom, ground	1 ½ teaspoons
Mitmita, optional	2 teaspoons
Salt	to taste
Turmeric, ground	½ tablespoon

Ethiopian Recipes

For many, participating in an Ethiopian meal is an exciting cultural experience: instead of using cutlery, plates, or serving dishes, the cook heaps components of the meal on a wheel of *injera*, a spongey bread that serves both as a "platter" and as a scoop for bites of vegetables or meat stew from the communal offering. Since eating by hand—the right hand—is traditional, a damp cloth or a fingerbowl is presented or available for all at the table. The food ranges from mild (vegetables and grains) to spicy or very spicy (the meats). Typical restaurant menu items include lentils and chickpeas for the grains; beans, tomatoes, yellow peas, peppers, cabbage, onions, spinach, and garlic for vegetables; chicken, lamb, and beef for meats; and shrimp and other fish for seafood.

Yebeg Alicha
Mild Lamb Stew

Ethiopian butter, or *niter kibbeh*, is found at any Ethiopian or international market and is sold online. Home cooks can use clarified butter—also known as ghee—and stir in the Ethiopian spice mixture, also sold online and at international markets.

Heat the oil in a large skillet over medium heat, and cook the onions until golden brown. Stir every 5 minutes so the onions cook evenly. Stir in the turmeric and then the lamb. Reduce the heat to medium low, and cover. Cook for about 5 minutes; stir in the garlic and salt. Cook for about 5 minutes more, and add the butter. Reduce the heat to low, cover, and cook until the meat is completely tender; stir slowly every 3 to 5 minutes. This process can take up to 30 minutes or longer, depending on the meat. Add the jalapeño peppers when it's ready to serve.

INGREDIENTS

SERVES 6

½ cup **canola oil**, or another vegetable oil

4 large **yellow onions**, peeled and diced

½ tablespoon **turmeric**, ground

2 pounds boneless **leg of lamb** (can also add ribs), cut into 2-inch cubes

2 or 3 heads **garlic**, peeled and minced

½ tablespoon **salt**

¼ cup **Ethiopian butter (niter kibbeh)** or **clarified butter** with spice mix

2 or 3 **jalapeño peppers**, sliced in half and seeded

Messer Wot

Spiced Lentils

This lentil dish calls for a popular Ethiopian spice mix called *berbere*, which contains chilis, allspice, and cinnamon, among other ingredients. It is available online, but many websites offer do-at-home recipes. You can vary the amount of berbere you add, depending on desired spiciness.

Make sure the rinse water for the lentils runs clear before you start to cook them. Serve this with injera, sold at local Ethiopian restaurants or homemade from an online injera bread kit. Otherwise, substitute large discs of pita bread.

1. Wash the lentils in warm water; then soak them in cold water until it is time to cook them. Heat the oil in a large saucepan over medium heat. Sauté the onions, stirring frequently, for about 5 minutes or until they turn golden. Add ½ cup of hot water and the berbere, and stir to mix well. If it appears too thick or dry, add more hot water. Cover the saucepan, and let the mixture cook for 2 minutes. Continue to add hot water, ¼ cup at a time, stirring after each addition. Continue cooking for about 10 minutes.

2. Drain the lentils; then add them back to the dry saucepan with 1 cup of fresh hot water, the minced garlic, and salt. Continue cooking until the lentils are soft, about 10 minutes more. Just before taking the saucepan off the heat, stir in the cardamom.

INGREDIENTS

SERVES 4

2 cups split **red lentils**, rinsed in warm water until clear

1 **red** or **yellow onion**, peeled and chopped

½ cup of **canola oil**

2 to 3 cups **hot water**

2 to 3 tablespoons **berbere**, or more

1 tablespoon **garlic**, minced

½ teaspoon **cardamom**, ground

Salt to taste

Ye'abesha Gomen Wat

Ethiopian Collard Greens

Heat the oil in a large saucepan over medium heat, and add the onion, cooking and stirring for about 5 minutes. When the onion starts to turn translucent, stir in the cardamom, and then add the collard greens. Mix well, reduce the heat to medium-low, and cover. Cook for about 5 minutes; then stir in the garlic and salt, cover, and cook for about 10 minutes more or until the collard greens start to change color. Stir in the mitmita (if using) and the jalapeño peppers. Remove from the heat, and let the mixtures rest for about 10 minutes before serving.

Mitmita is a hot Ethiopian spice made from ground chilis, onions, ginger, herbs, and salt. This is available for sale online or at specialty spice stores.

INGREDIENTS
SERVES 4

½ cup **canola** or **olive oil**

1 large **red onion**, peeled and diced

1 teaspoon **cardamom**, ground

2 pounds frozen **collard greens**, thawed and chopped, or 2 pounds fresh, rinsed, trimmed, and chopped

1 head **garlic**, peeled and cloves minced

1 tablespoon or less **salt**

2 teaspoons **mitmita** (optional) (see note)

2 large **jalapeño peppers**, seeded and chopped

Lab

Ethiopian Cottage Cheese and Yogurt Dessert

Typically, Ethiopians do not eat sweets at the end of a meal, choosing instead to serve platters of fresh fruit and a dairy-based mixture of cottage cheese and yogurt. This is served on top of flat bread.

Combine all the ingredients in a large bowl, and mix well. Drain off any excess liquid so the mixture is dry enough to stay firm when served but moist enough to spoon out. Serve on toasted flat bread.

INGREDIENTS
MAKES 1 QUART

1 pound small-curd **cottage cheese** or **farmer's cheese**

4 tablespoons **plain yogurt**

2 tablespoons fresh **parsley**, minced

1 tablespoon grated **lemon zest**

1 teaspoon **salt**

¼ teaspoon **black pepper**

Prayer to

ST. FRUMENTIUS

Pray for us, dear Frumentius, that we may also
"bloom where we are planted." You were just a
young boy in a strange and pagan land, but you
made the best of the situation and brought truth
and life to that desolate land and lost people.
We pray for your intercession that we may bring
the light of Christ with us wherever we go in the
hope of inspiring others to follow Him.
In His name we pray. Amen.

— Used with permission from CatholicExchange.com

NOVEMBER

SAINTLY MEAL *for* NOVEMBER

ST. MARTIN DE PORRES

A Traditional Peruvian Meal

Papas a la Huancaina
Potatoes with Yellow Chilis and Cheese Sauce

Ceviche a la Peruana
Peruvian Ceviche

Arroz con Leche
Rice with Milk

ST. MARTIN DE PORRES

NOVEMBER 3

Born: 1579	Died: 1639	Patron saint of African Americans, barbers, innkeepers, and race relations

Born in Lima, Peru, St. Martin de Porres was the illegitimate son of a Spanish nobleman and a freed slave, possibly of African descent. While he was still a youngster, his father abandoned and disowned him, leaving him in poverty. When St. Martin was about twelve years old, he was taken on by a barber to learn the trade. He was often ridiculed by others for being of mixed race. Nonetheless, he was a devout Christian, spending hours in daily prayer. He was accepted first as a volunteer with the Dominicans of Holy Rosary Priory in Lima, and when he turned fifteen, he was admitted to the convent. He worked there for many years at different humble tasks.

Eight years later, at the age of twenty-four, St. Martin became a member of the Third Order of Saint Dominic. Ten years later, he was assigned to oversee the infirmary. He had a deep-seated compassion for the sick and the poor, regardless of their race or color. He even brought them off the streets of Lima and placed them in his own bed. These actions underscored his great love for God. St. Martin de Porres experienced bilocation and levitation and had the ability to produce instant cures for the sick.

St. Martin de Porres was beatified in 1837 by Pope Gregory XVI and was canonized in 1962 by Pope John XXIII.

SHOPPING LIST

BAKING SUPPLIES

Sugar, granulated | 1 cup

BREAD

Crackers, such as
Saltines | 4 plus more as needed

CONDIMENTS

Vegetable oil | 2 tablespoons

DAIRY

Eggs | 2

Queso fresco or
white **farmer's cheese** | 2 cups

Whole milk or **nonfat milk** | 2 cups

DRY GOODS

Raisins | ½ cup

Rice, long grain | 1 cup

PRODUCE

**Aji amarillo,
aji rocoto,
serrano chile,** or
habanero chile | 1

Cilantro | 1 bunch

Garlic | 1 or 2 heads

Lettuce | 2 heads

Limes | 15 to 20

Onion, red | 1

Potatoes, white or yellow | 8

Yellow chiles | 3 or 4

SEAFOOD

Sea bass, sole, or **flounder**,
high quality | 2 pounds

SPICES

Black pepper | to taste

Cinnamon, ground | to taste

Cinnamon sticks | 2

Salt | to taste

Vanilla extract | 1 teaspoon,
or more to taste

Whole cloves | 4 or 5

Peruvian Recipes

Peruvian food gets its character from many ethnic backgrounds. Immigrants from China, Japan, West Africa, Italy, Spain, and Germany, plus its own indigenous Incan roots have contributed to it. Each incoming group has cooked with the local crops of corn, potatoes, and beans to shape homey dishes that also included their own favorite ingredients, from chicken and pork to wheat, barley, rice, lentils, eggplant, apples, oranges, vinegar, and assorted herbs and spices.

Besides the ethnic differences, Peru offers a diverse geography and topography, from the mountainous areas of the Andes to the plains to the Amazon rainforest to the coastal areas that rely on seafood—hence the classic seafood dish *ceviche*. Visitors to Peruvian restaurants may not even know where to begin, since most offerings contain familiar ingredients and are tempting.

Papas a la Huancaina

Potatoes with Yellow Chile and Cheese Sauce

Papas a la Huancaina is a dish of sliced boiled potatoes covered with a white farmer's cheese sauce that is typically served cold as a first course or as a luncheon dish. Most well-stocked supermarkets carry farmer's cheese; a good substitute for the yellow chile (*aji Amarillo*), a native of Peru, is the serrano chile. If you desire, you may add minced garlic to the sauce.

1. Heat a large pot of salted water over medium heat, and bring it to a boil; add the potatoes. Cook for about 20 minutes or until they are fork tender. Drain, and let cool.

2. To make the huancaina sauce, put the oil and chiles into a food processor or blender, and process. Add the evaporated milk, and blend. Add the cheese and crackers, and blend until smooth. The sauce should be thick; if it is too thin, add more crackers.

3. To serve, place lettuce leaves on a serving dish, slice and place the potatoes on top of the lettuce, and drizzle with the sauce. Slice the boiled eggs, and place on top. Decorate with the black olives. Serve cooled or at room temperature.

INGREDIENTS

SERVES 4 TO 6

8 yellow or white **potatoes**, peeled

Lettuce leaves for serving

2 hard-boiled **eggs**

8 large **black olives**, pitted and halved

HUANCAINA SAUCE

2 tablespoons **vegetable oil**

3 or 4 **yellow chiles**, seeded and chopped

2 cups white **farmer's cheese** (queso fresco)

4 **crackers**

¾ cup **evaporated milk**

Salt to taste

Lettuce leaves for serving

Ceviche a la Peruana

Ceviche

Ceviche, also spelled *seviche*, is a popular Latin American, Mexican, and Spanish dish made from raw seafood that gets "cooked" by the lime juice. Different cooks use various types of hot chiles. Peruvian cooks often select the aji amarillo or aji rocoto, which can be very fiery. Another option is a habanero. If your local market does not carry the aji rocoto, it is available online. For tamer flavors, use serrano or jalapeño chiles instead. For an authentic Peruvian taste, serve the ceviche with Peruvian *cancha* (toasted corn kernels), available online.

1. Rinse the fish with cold water, and cut into 1-inch cubes. Place in a glass dish. Add the onion, chile, garlic, salt, and pepper. Pour the lime juice over the ingredients to cover them completely. Seal with plastic wrap, and refrigerate for at least 5 hours.

2. Remove the wrap, add the cilantro, and toss gently. Place on lettuce leaves, and serve.

INGREDIENTS

SERVES 6 TO 8

2 pounds very fresh and high-quality **white fish**, such as sea bass, sole, or flounder

1 **red onion**, peeled, quartered, and thinly sliced

1 **aji amarillo**, or **aji rocoto** (hotter), or **habanero chile**, seeds and veins removed, and diced

6 to 8 cloves **garlic**, peeled and minced, or to taste

Salt and freshly ground **black pepper** to taste

Juice from 15 to 20 fresh **limes**, enough to cover the fish

Small bunch **cilantro**, washed and chopped

Lettuce leaves for serving

Arroz con Leche

Rice with Milk

Peruvians have made their own version of the popular "rice with milk" Spanish dessert. It may even be sweeter and richer than the Spanish version, especially when made with condensed or evaporated milk, or both.

1. Place 2 cups of water, the rice, cinnamon, and cloves in a large saucepan, and soak the rice for about 30 minutes, or longer.

2. Place the saucepan over medium heat, and bring to a boil. Reduce the heat to medium low, add the milk, and continue cooking, stirring often to prevent sticking. Add the sugar and vanilla, and cook for about 15 minutes or until the rice is tender. Sprinkle raisins and cinnamon on top when serving.

INGREDIENTS

SERVES 4 TO 6

1 cup uncooked **long-grain rice**, such as Basmati

2 **cinnamon sticks**

4 or 5 **whole cloves**

2 cups **whole** or **nonfat milk**

1 cup **granulated sugar**

1 teaspoon **vanilla extract**, or more to taste

½ cup **raisins**

Cinnamon, ground, for sprinkling

A Prayer to
ST. MARTIN DE PORRES

To you, St. Martin de Porres, we prayerfully
lift up our hearts filled with serene confidence
and devotion. Mindful of your unbounded
and helpful charity to all levels of society
and also of your meekness and humility
of heart, we offer our petitions to you.

Pour out upon our families the precious gifts
of your solicitous and generous intercession;
show to the people of every race and every
color the paths of unity and of justice; implore
from our Father in heaven the coming of His
kingdom, so that through mutual benevolence
in God men may increase the fruits of grace
and merit the rewards of eternal life. Amen.

—Used with permission from CatholicCulture.org

NOVEMBER 4

ST. CHARLES BORROMEO

—*Italy*—

Born: 1538, Died: 1584

St. Charles Borromeo was the descendant of Italian nobility with great wealth. Despite his ties to nobility, he wanted only to serve the Church. When his uncle Cardinal de Medici became pope, he appointed St. Charles a cardinal deacon in charge of the Archdiocese of Milan. In 1563, St. Charles decided to enter the priesthood and, in 1565, was appointed the archbishop of Milan.

He took steps to dramatically reform the city, which had slid into an abyss of corruption. St. Charles discovered clergy selling indulgences. He also found that many clergy were ignoring or were unaware of basic Church teachings. His reforms included founding seminaries and universities to educate aspiring clergy in preparation for the priesthood.

BRENNAN'S BAKED APPLES

St. Charles Borromeo is the patron not only of bishops, catechists, and cardinals but also of apple orchards. It is fitting, then, to honor him with baked apples. At Brennan's in New Orleans, these are served as a brunch item with a brown sugar–honey sauce. With a scoop of vanilla ice cream, they also make a great dessert.

1. Combine all the filling ingredients in a mixing bowl. Using the paddle attachment of a standing mixer, blend the ingredients on medium speed for about 4 minutes. Store the mixture in the refrigerator for at least a few hours before using.

2. When you are ready to bake the apples, preheat the oven to 350 degrees. Wash the apples, and trim the bottom of each so that it sits flat. Remove each core with an apple corer.

3. Next, using your hands, roll about 2 tablespoons of the pecan-oat mixture into a ball, flatten it slightly, and place it on top of one apple. Avoid stuffing the apple with the filling. Repeat for the remaining apples.

4. Place the apples in a baking dish. Fill the dish with ½ inch of hot water. Bake for 40 minutes. Keep an eye on the apples; if the tops start to get too crisp or brown, cover them with aluminum foil to prevent further browning. Poke a few small holes in the foil to allow steam to escape. The apples should be fork tender but not mushy.

5. Meanwhile, combine all the sauce ingredients except the butter in a saucepan. Bring to a boil, and cook for 2 minutes. Remove from the heat, and add the diced butter, stirring until well incorporated. Pour the sauce over the cooked apples, and serve warm.

It is important to use a variety of apple that will retain its shape and texture during extended cooking. If Honeycrisp is unavailable, you may substitute Granny Smith.

INGREDIENTS

SERVES 10

PECAN-OAT FILLING

½ cup **pecan pieces**

½ cup **rolled oats**

¼ cup **unsalted butter**, at room temperature

¼ cup **raisins**

¼ cup **light brown sugar**

3 tablespoons **all-purpose flour**

½ teaspoon **cinnamon**, ground

10 **Honeycrisp apples**

BROWN SUGAR SAUCE

1 cup **light brown sugar**

¼ cup **honey**

3 tablespoons **water**

⅛ teaspoon **vanilla extract**

Pinch **salt**

½ cup plus 2 tablespoons **unsalted butter**, diced

NOVEMBER 13
(Feast Day, Eastern)

ST. JOHN CHRYSOSTOM
— Turkey —

Born: 344 or 347, Died: 407

Honored by the Catholic, Eastern Orthodox, and Anglican faiths, St. John Chrysostom left behind a legacy of insightful teachings, earning him the title of Doctor of the Church.

Around 367, St. John met Bishop Meletius, who inspired the youth to study Scripture and lead an ascetic life. St. John became a hermit, living a rigorous life dedicated to prayer and to memorizing the Bible. When he was ordained to the priesthood, his straightforward, practical preaching earned him fame among the locals. But it also earned him enmity.

St. John's vocal opposition to extravagance within the clergy and the upper classes led to his exile. He was never allowed to return to Constantinople.

PATLICANLI KEBAP
Eggplant Kebab with Yogurt-Marinated Chicken

SERVES 6

ACCORDING TO TURKISH COOK OZLEM WARREN, this Southern Turkish dish features eggplants, chicken, yogurt, and assorted seasonings that yield an intensely tempting kebab dinner. A native of southern Turkey, Ms. Warren explained that dishes that feature meat cooked with vegetables in trays are considered kebabs and were traditionally cooked in bakeries. "Another example is the Traybake kebab," she said. "My grandmother would prep the mixture, and we would take it to the local bakery to bake it for us." Serve the dish hot with plain rice or bulgur pilaf.

 Turkish hot red pepper paste is available online and at well-stocked international markets.

FOR THE KEBABS

1. Preheat the oven to 350 degrees. Peel the eggplants in strips, using a vegetable peeler or a small knife. Slice the eggplants in half lengthwise; then cut them into ¼-inch-thick slices. Place the slices on a tray, and sprinkle them with salt to extract bitter juices. Set aside for 15 minutes.

2. Place the chicken pieces in a large bowl. Stir in 1 tablespoon of olive oil, the yogurt, garlic, tomato paste, red pepper paste (if using), red pepper flakes, and salt and pepper. Mix the chicken pieces with the marinade. Cover the chicken, and chill for at least 30 minutes; this can be prepared the night before.

3. Pat the excess water off the eggplants with paper towels. Place the slices on a baking sheet, drizzle them with 3 tablespoons of olive oil, and place them in the preheated oven. Bake for 15 minutes.

KEBAB INGREDIENTS

2 medium **eggplants**

Salt

1 ½ pounds **boneless chicken thighs** or **chicken breasts**, skinned and cut into 1½-inch cubes

6 tablespoons **olive oil**

2 tablespoons plain **whole-milk yogurt**

2 **garlic** cloves, peeled and minced

½ tablespoon **tomato paste**

½ tablespoon **Turkish hot pepper paste** (optional)

Red pepper flakes to taste

2 red **romano** or **bell peppers**, seeded and sliced into chunks

1 **green bell pepper**, seeded and sliced into chunks

1 medium **onion**, peeled and coarsely chopped

Salt and freshly ground **black pepper** to taste

4. Meanwhile, heat the remaining olive oil in a large skillet over medium heat. Add the chicken pieces, and sauté for 4 to 5 minutes. Turn off the heat. Reserve pan and juices for step 1 below.

5. In an oven-proof baking dish, place the chicken pieces side by side with the onion, alternating red and green pepper chunks, and eggplant pieces. Repeat this by layering the ingredients in this order. Place any remaining eggplant pieces on top.

FOR THE SAUCE

1. To make the sauce, stir the red pepper paste and the tomato paste with 1½ cups of water in the skillet used for cooking the chicken. Pour this mixture over the chicken and eggplant mixture.

2. Bake at 350 degrees for 35 to 40 minutes or until the chicken and vegetables are cooked through and the chicken has turned a pale golden color. Serve hot.

SAUCE INGREDIENTS

½ tablespoon **red pepper paste** or 1 to 2 teaspoon **red pepper flakes**

½ tablespoon **tomato paste**

NOVEMBER 17

ST. ELIZABETH

— *Hungary* —

Born: circa 1207, Died: 1231

The daughter of a Hungarian king, St. Elizabeth led a short but noble life. Married at age fourteen, she bore three children with her husband Louis of Thuringia. To help the poor, she distributed alms and built a hospital in honor of St. Francis of Assisi. She received Franciscan instruction, shaping her life into one of chastity and prayer.

St. Elizabeth was widowed at age twenty when Louis died in the sixth Crusade. Afterward, she joined the Third Order of Saint Francis, spending her days with the poor in the hospital she had founded. Suffering from ill health, St. Elizabeth died at age twenty-four. Miracles of healing were reported to have happened at her grave site.

GULYÁSLEVES
Hungarian Goulash Soup with Pinched Spaetzle

Tracing the origins of Hungary's robust dish, a national favorite, could take food historians back as far as the ninth century and the Magyar shepherds. Most sources agree that the Hungarian cowherds, often in the plains for months at a time, assembled its original version. When one of the cattle died, the cowherds mixed its meat with lard, onions, water, salt, and paprika, creating a soup or stew that has been refined over the years. Indeed, the word *gulyas* means "cowherd" or "herdsman." It is noteworthy that the original soup or stew now has countless variations—and apparently each restaurant cook or housewife thinks his or her dish is the best. What the ancient herdsmen assembled has now become not only a Hungarian staple but also an international star. It is also considered a soup, not a stew.

FOR THE SOUP

1. Heat the oil in a large Dutch oven over medium heat, and sauté the onions until golden. Stir in the paprika, tomato, and wax peppers; cook about 10 minutes.

2. Add the celeriac root, peppercorns, carrots, and meat, and cook until the meat starts to brown.

3. Add 4 to 6 cups of water. Cover, and cook over medium heat for about 20 minutes; then add the potatoes.

4. Cook until the meat is tender, about 1½ hours. Add extra water, as needed.

If celeriac is not available, use 2 or 3 stalks of celery. Use firm-flesh potatoes, such as russets.

SOUP INGREDIENTS

SERVES 6

2 tablespoons **vegetable oil**

1 large **onion**, peeled and chopped

2 tablespoons **Hungarian paprika**, ground

1 ripe **tomato**, diced

2 **Hungarian wax peppers**, sliced

1 small **celeriac root**, thinly sliced (see note)

10 to 12 whole **black peppercorns**

4 **carrots**, peeled and chopped

1 pound **beef roast**, cut into 1-inch cubes

1 pound **boneless pork roast**, cut into 1-inch cubes

5 to 6 medium **potatoes**, peeled and sliced (see note)

Salt to taste

FOR THE PINCHED SPAETZLE (CSIPETKE)

Csipetke, or pinched spaetzle, are considered a cross between a pasta and a dumpling. These are popular add-ons to soups and stews, particularly to goulash. Katalin Gimes always cooks them in boiling water, not in the soup, to maintain the texture and to prevent murkiness in the soup liquid. Add a handful to each plate.

1. Mix the flour and salt. Add the eggs. Stir to make a stiff dough, sprinkling in a few drops of cold water at a time, if necessary. Knead until smooth. Cover the dough, and let it rest at least 30 minutes.

2. Flatten the dough a bit at a time between floured palms (or roll ⅛ inch thick on a floured board), and pinch off pieces slightly smaller than a dime. Drop all the spaetzle at once into rapidly boiling salted water; cook until tender, about 15 minutes.

3. Drain the spaetzle in a colander, and briefly rinse them with warm water. Once the water has dripped off, place them in a bowl, coat them with oil, and set aside in a warm place until ready to use.

1 cup **all-purpose flour**

½ teaspoon **salt**

2 large **eggs**

2 tablespoons **cold water**, or more as needed

1 tablespoon **vegetable oil**

NOVEMBER 24

ST. ANDREW DŨNG-LẠC

— Vietnam —

Born: 1795, Died: 1839

A native of North Vietnam, St. Andrew Dũng-Lạc was ordained in 1823 and was a holy, effective diocesan priest, bringing many into the Faith.

In 1832, the emperor began persecuting Christians, demanding that they renounce their Faith. To avoid persecution, St. Andrew changed his name to Dũng-Lạc and moved to a different part of the country. Arrested, freed, and rearrested with a fellow priest, the two were taken to Hanoi, where they were brutalized and finally beheaded on December 21, 1839. St. Andrew was among 117 who were martyred between 1820 and 1862. In all, more than 100,000 were martyred from the sixteenth century until the 1860s. Reputedly, the brutality was among the worst in history.

GOI DU DU
Green Papaya Salad

SERVES 6

VIETNAMESE, THAI, AND LAOTIAN COOKS use a popular staple, the green papaya, in what has become a traditional side dish with seafood and beef entrées. Finding green papayas, however, requires a trip to an Asian or international market. Green papaya is often sold shredded, but it should be used the same day. A better option is to pick out a whole one without blemishes or soft spots. Before shredding, slice off the stem end, then peel off the skin with a sharp knife or potato peeler, cut the papaya in half, and remove the seeds. To shred the papaya easily, use a large four-sided box grater.

1. Combine the dressing ingredients, and set aside.

2. To fry fresh shallots, pour a generous amount of vegetable oil into a medium-size skillet. Heat the oil; then add the shallots, and fry, stirring often, for 6 minutes or until browned. Remove the shallots with a slotted spoon, and place them on paper towels to drain.

3. Optional: Place the peanuts in the same skillet, and roast them briefly in the hot oil, about 3 minutes. Remove the peanuts with a slotted spoon, and place them on paper towels to drain.

4. Add the shrimp and chilis (if using) to the remaining hot oil in the skillet, and sauté, stirring often, until a fork pressed onto a shrimp bounces back easily, about 5 minutes.

5. Place the salad on a serving plate. Arrange the shrimp and chilis on top of the salad, and garnish with the fried shallots, peanuts, and cilantro leaves. Serve with more dressing, if desired.

 Many varieties of fish sauce are available, but they are fairly similar. Thai fish sauce will work fine in this recipe.

Fried shallots are sold online, and at some supermarkets and Asian markets.

DRESSING INGREDIENTS

1 tablespoon **lime juice**, preferably fresh

1 ½ tablespoons **sugar**

½ teaspoon **fish sauce** (see note)

SALAD INGREDIENTS

1 pound **green papaya**, shredded into narrow strips

2 tablespoons **Thai basil leaves**, minced

2 tablespoons **mint leaves**, minced

½ to 1 teaspoon **salt**

2 tablespoons **fried shallots** or 3 **shallots**, peeled and thinly sliced (see note)

2 tablespoons **peanuts**, coarsely ground

1 pound medium **shrimp**, peeled and deveined

Fresh **chilis**, chopped, to taste (optional)

3 tablespoons **cilantro leaves**

DECEMBER

DECEMBER 3

ST. FRANCIS XAVIER

— India —

Born: 1506, Died: 1552

At the time St. Francis Xavier became a priest, Portugal was colonizing India. St. Francis was chosen to go to the colony of Goa and formally represent the Church there. His duties included tending to the sick and working with the Christian Goans who were unfamiliar with their Faith. St. Francis spent several years in Goa, overseeing the building of at least forty churches.

St. Francis also evangelized for some time in Japan. The next destination for his missionary work was China. The sea voyage was difficult, and the Chinese border had been closed to foreigners. St. Francis, who had become very ill, was put ashore on an island just a few miles from China, which he never reached.

CHICKEN CURRY

INDIA'S STATE OF GOA ON THE SUBCONTINENT'S WEST COAST features meals based on such staples as coconut, seafood, pork, rice, chilis, and assorted spices. Over the ages, the Hindus, Muslims, and Portuguese Catholic colonists have shaped today's Goan cuisine.

One of the staples of the Goan family table is a chicken curry. For the best flavor, use fresh and freshly ground spices. Serve with rice, and garnish with sprigs of cilantro.

1. Heat the vegetable oil in a large saucepan over medium-high heat; add the onion, and sauté until soft and lightly golden.

2. Stir in the tomatoes, and cook until most of the liquid has evaporated.

3. Add the chicken, and cook for about 5 minutes or until cooked through.

4. Add the spices, vinegar, and brown sugar, and cook for about 5 minutes.

5. Add the coconut milk, garlic, and ginger, and bring to a boil.

6. Reduce the heat to low, and cook for about 20 minutes or until the sauce has thickened slightly.

7. Adjust the seasonings, and add the chilis and salt as needed.

8. Serve over rice prepared according to package directions. Garnish with cilantro sprigs before serving, if desired.

INGREDIENTS
SERVES 4 TO 6

3 tablespoons **vegetable oil**

2 **onions**, peeled and diced

2 or 3 large **tomatoes**, chopped

4 pounds **boneless chicken thighs**, cut into cubes

2 tablespoons **cilantro**, ground

1 tablespoon **cumin**, ground

2 teaspoons **turmeric**, ground

2 teaspoons **salt**

1 teaspoon **cloves**, ground

2 tablespoons **vinegar**

1 tablespoon **brown sugar**

¾ cup **coconut milk**

5 **garlic cloves**, peeled and crushed

1-inch piece fresh **ginger**, peeled and sliced

2 dried **red chilis**, or more as desired

Salt to taste

Cilantro sprigs for garnish (optional)

DECEMBER 7

ST. AMBROSE

—*Italy*—

Born: circa 340, Died: 397

St. Ambrose grew up in a Roman Christian family. According to legend, when St. Ambrose was an infant, a swarm of bees landed on his face, leaving behind a drop of honey. That convinced his father that his son would become a great orator with a "honeyed tongue."

St. Ambrose was consecrated bishop of Milan in 374. During his tenure, he accomplished great things for the Church, including influencing St. Augustine of Hippo to convert to Christianity; disallowing several basilicas to be ceded to the Arians; and delivering sermons and important theological treatises that impacted the lives of several popes and the public at large. He is one of the four original Doctors of the Church.

ANCIENT ROMAN HONEY CAKE

ACCORDING TO A CHRONICLER OF EARLY CHURCH HISTORY, St. Ambrose noted that his faithful Christians lived like busy bees, likening the Church to a beehive. That could explain how St. Ambrose's legacy has generated so many honey-based recipes, with many dating back to medieval kitchens.

To mirror the original recipe, try substituting spelt flour, available at well-stocked supermarkets or health food stores. It is closest in results to the flour Romans used, but using all-purpose flour is fine, too. Serve slices of the honey cake with pure honey, plain or vanilla Greek yogurt, and jam or marmalade made from citrus and berries.

1. Preheat the oven to 350 degrees. Use baking spray to prepare a 10-inch round cake pan, and set aside.

2. Mix the dry ingredients together in a mixing bowl. In a separate bowl, combine and beat together the liquid ingredients. Slowly beat the liquid ingredients into the dry ingredients, and pour into the prepared pan.

3. Bake for 30 to 40 minutes or until a toothpick inserted in the center of the cake comes out clean. Remove the cake from the oven, and cool before serving.

INGREDIENTS
SERVES 8 TO 12

1 ½ cups **all-purpose flour**

1 ½ teaspoons **baking soda**

½ teaspoon **salt**

¾ cup **milk**

¾ cup **honey**

1 large **egg**

½ cup **vegetable oil**, **olive oil**, or a mix of both

1 teaspoon **lemon juice**

The top of the cake may darken quickly, so cover it with foil after 20 minutes of baking time.

SAINTLY MEAL *for* DECEMBER

OUR LADY OF GUADALUPE

A Mexican Feast

Arroz de mi Madre
My Mother's Rice

Tostadas con Frijoles
Bean Tostadas

Enchiladas de Queso con Chile Rojo
Red Chile Cheese Enchiladas

Guacamole

Pastel Tres Leches
Three-Milk Cake

OUR LADY OF GUADALUPE

DECEMBER 12

Celebrating the feast of Our Lady of Guadalupe is popular in Mexico and elsewhere. Parties, festivals, and special dishes help people to remember the miracle of Our Lady of Guadalupe.

Historical accounts relate that in 1531 a native peasant and convert to Catholicism, Juan Diego, was walking by Tepeyac Hill in Mexico City when he heard a woman call out to him. A lady who looked like a native princess, dressed in shining garb, introduced herself as the "Immaculate Mother of God." She asked Juan Diego to ask the local bishop to have a chapel built at the location of her apparition.

The bishop rejected Juan Diego's message twice but promised to listen to his request if he returned with evidence of this vision. On her third visit, Juan Diego told the Virgin of the bishop's request. Our Lady instructed Juan Diego to fill his tilma (cloak) with the flowers he would find on top of the hill and carry them to the bishop. To his surprise, Juan Diego found roses growing on the hill, even though it was winter. Our Lady arranged them in his tilma, and he brought them to the bishop. When Juan Diego opened his tilma, the roses fell out, and the Virgin's image was miraculously imprinted on the tilma.

The chapel was built, and the tilma was hung over the altar. Our Lady's image and the tilma remain intact. Over the centuries, many mysteries have been discovered in the image on the tilma and have drawn millions of worshippers to Our Lady of Guadalupe's basilica in what is today a suburb of Mexico City.

SHOPPING LIST

BAKING SUPPLIES

All-purpose flour	1 ½ cups
Baking powder	1 teaspoon
Sugar, granulated	3 tablespoons

BREAD

Corn tortillas	24

CANNED GOODS

Chicken broth	2 to 4 cups or more, as needed
Evaporated milk	one 12-ounce can
Sweetened condensed milk	one 14-ounce can
Refried beans (or make fresh)	two 15-ounce cans
Tomato sauce	one 15-ounce can

CONDIMENTS

Canola oil	2 to 3 tablespoons plus
Vegetable oil	¼ cup plus 2 tablespoons

DAIRY

Monterey Jack cheese, shredded	2 cups
Monterey Jack and cheddar cheese, shredded	3 cups
Eggs	4 large
Sour cream	1 cup
Whipping/heavy cream	2 ¼ cup
Whole milk	1 ½ cups

DRY GOODS

Dried red chiles	20
Pinto beans	2 cups
Rice, medium to short grain	1 cup

PRODUCE

Avocados	6
Cilantro	2 bunches
Garlic	3 heads
Jalapeño peppers	3
Lettuce, Iceberg	½ head
Limes	5
Onion, white	2
Scallions	4 or 5
Strawberries or kiwi (optional)	garnish for cake
Tomatoes	7 large
Tomatoes, cherry	6 to 8

MISCELLANEOUS

Grand Marnier (optional)	3 tablespoons

SPICES

Black pepper	to taste
Cinnamon, ground	to taste
Cumin, ground	to taste
Salt	to taste
Vanilla extract	2 teaspoons

Mexican Recipes

Mexican cuisine may have its roots in early Mayan days, when corn and beans were dietary staples. Even the later centuries of the Aztecs—who added chiles, domesticated fowls, and chocolate to their menus—continued to shape the cuisine. As explorers from Spain arrived, with their staples of garlic, spices, and dairy, the Mexican kitchen began to resemble what modern Mexicans enjoy. Mexican recipes generally rely on the basics of corn, beans, chiles, garlic, and cilantro to shape the flavors that people classify as Mexican.

Arroz de mi Madre

My Mother's Rice

Rice is a popular side dish throughout Mexico, but its presentation differs between northern and southern recipes. White rice prevails in the south, but northern cooks perk up the dish with the addition of tomatoes, onions or scallions, garlic, and chicken broth after the rice is browned in oil. Home cooks can decide to season their rice, and they often use cilantro and ground cumin.

Heat the oil in a large stockpot or skillet over medium heat, and add the rice. Sauté the rice, stirring often, until it turns a pale golden color. Stir in the garlic and scallions; add the tomato sauce and enough broth to cover the rice by about 2 inches, and stir. Then stir in the fresh cilantro, ground cumin, and salt and pepper to taste. Cover the pot, and reduce the heat to very low. Cook until the rice is tender, about 20 minutes.

INGREDIENTS
SERVES 4 TO 6

2 to 3 tablespoons **canola oil** for frying

1 cup uncooked medium- to short-grain **rice**

2 **garlic cloves**, peeled and minced

3 **scallions**, thinly sliced, white and light green tops only

One 15-ounce can **tomato sauce**

2 to 4 cups **chicken broth**, or more as needed

½ bunch fresh **cilantro**, chopped

Cumin, ground, to taste

Salt and freshly ground **black pepper** to taste

Tostadas con Frijoles

Bean Tostadas

A tostada—translated "toasted"—is a crispy deep-fried corn tortilla with a topping of beans, meat, and vegetables or with just a single topping. Note: Use canned frijoles, or follow the recipe below for a homemade version.

1. Heat about 2 tablespoons of vegetable oil in a skillet, and heat the beans until warm throughout, stirring often. Set the beans aside.

2. In a clean skillet, add about ¼ cup oil, and heat over medium heat. Fry the tortillas in the oil one at a time, turning over once when one side becomes golden, about 30 seconds per side. Remove from the heat, and drain on paper towels.

3. To serve, take one tostada, spread a spoonful of mashed beans over it, and then sprinkle on the lettuce, tomatoes, and cheese. Eat by picking up the tostada with both hands.

INGREDIENTS

SERVES 6

Two 15-ounce cans **refried beans (frijoles)**

Vegetable oil for frying

12 corn **tortillas**

½ head **iceberg lettuce**, thinly sliced

2 **tomatoes**, chopped

2 cups **cheddar** or **Monterey Jack cheese**, or both, shredded

2 cups fresh **salsa** (see the recipe on the next page)

Frijoles Refritos

Refried Beans

Refried beans are readily available canned, but following a traditional recipe from scratch produces a flavor-packed dish. This may be time-consuming, as the beans require overnight soaking to soften, but the end result is worth it. For more flavor, you may add pork or bacon to the beans while cooking them.

1. Rinse the soaked beans thoroughly in cold water until the water runs clear, removing stones or sand if needed. Remove broken pieces of beans, if preferred. Place the beans in a large pot, and add the garlic, onion, and jalapeño pepper. Add cold water until the pot is half full. Add salt to taste.

2. Bring the water to a boil; then turn the heat to low and cook the beans until fork tender, 1½ to 2 hours. If needed, add more hot water to cover the beans by about 2 inches. Continue cooking, and add salt to taste.

3. When cooked, reserve some of the liquid. Remove the onion, garlic, and jalapeño pepper if you prefer. Mash the beans well, and add the reserved liquid, if needed, to keep the beans moist.

INGREDIENTS

SERVES 6

2 cups dry **pinto beans**, soaked overnight

1 clove **garlic**, peeled

½ **white onion**, peeled

1 **jalapeño pepper**, stemmed and whole or seeded

Salt to taste

Roasted Green Chiles *(for Fresh Salsa)*

Roasting green chiles is simple but time-consuming. We recommend that you make a whole batch and store the leftovers in the refrigerator or freezer. They can be roasted over an open flame, such as a grill, and even in a very hot pan on the stove, but the safest method is to place them under a broiler. These instructions apply to many kinds of green spicy chiles (4 to 9 inches long), although our recipe calls for Anaheim chiles.

INGREDIENTS

Anaheim or other **green spicy chiles**, as many as you will be roasting

1. Heat the broiler. Line a rimmed baking sheet with aluminum foil.

2. Wash the chiles, and pat them dry.

3. Arrange the chiles on the baking sheet. They can touch each other but shouldn't lie on top of each other.

4. Once the broiler is hot, place the baking sheet on the top rack. Keep the oven door slightly ajar to watch the chiles' skin blistering and charring. This usually takes about 10 minutes. Check every 3 to 4 minutes. Rotate the pan as needed

5. Remove the baking sheet from the oven, and using tongs, turn the chiles once before repeating step 4. The chiles do not need to be completely black all over; some brown spots may remain.

6. Remove the chiles from the oven, and, using the tongs, place them in sealable bags, filling the bags about half full. Close the bags tightly, and let the chiles steam for 30 minutes.

7. Protecting your hands (and anything you might touch afterward) with gloves, remove the chiles from the bags, and peel off the skin. The skin should peel easily, but if it sticks in places, you can run warm water over it while peeling.

8. Once all the skin has been removed, still wearing gloves, slice the chiles in half, and carefully scrape out the seeds with a spoon and discard. Try not to run water over the chiles to remove errant seeds, as this will remove the flavorful oil from the chiles.

9. Cut off the stems, and either continue to prepare for your recipe or store. They can be stored diced or in larger pieces in the refrigerator for about 4 days or in the freezer for up to two months.

10. Discard gloves without touching them on the outside or touching your face, and immediately wash your hands with detergent or soap to remove the oil.

Fresh Salsa

Combine all the ingredients in a food processor or blender, and blend together until chunky. Adjust seasoning with more fresh lime juice, if desired.

INGREDIENTS
SERVES 4 TO 6

5 large **tomatoes** or one 15-ounce can **plum tomatoes**.

6 to 8 **cherry tomatoes**

½ **onion**, peeled and chopped, or several **green onions**, chopped

Fresh **garlic**, chopped, to taste

4 roasted **Anaheim green chiles** or 1 **jalapeño pepper**

Salt and freshly ground **black pepper** to taste

Juice from 1 **lime**, or more as needed

Enchiladas de Queso con Chile Rojo

Red Chile Cheese Enchiladas

1. Preheat the oven to 300 degrees. Line a rimmed baking sheet with foil, and spray it with nonstick cooking spray. Set aside.

2. Heat several tablespoons of oil in a large skillet over medium heat, and fry each tortilla lightly until soft. Lay the corn tortillas out flat on the cookie sheet, and sprinkle with the onions and shredded cheese. Roll each up tightly, and pour the sauce over the top. Bake for 15 minutes or until all the cheese melts. Top with dollop of sour cream and a pinch of chopped cilantro.

INGREDIENTS
SERVES 6 TO 8

Canola oil for frying

12 **corn tortillas**

1 cup **onion**, finely chopped (optional)

3 cups cheese, a mixture of **Monterey Jack** and **Cheddar**, shredded

2 cups **red enchilada sauce** (see the recipe on the next page)

Sour cream for serving

Fresh **cilantro**, finely chopped, for serving

Red Sauce for Enchiladas

1. Put the chilis in a large stockpot with water to cover. Bring to a boil over medium heat, and cook until the chiles are softened and the color changes to pale red.

2. Place several chiles in a blender or food processor with some cooking liquid. Add the garlic and the onion, and process until smooth. Add the remaining chiles, and process again.

3. Add salt to taste.

4. Pour the mixture into a skillet, and heat over low heat until ready to use.

 You will get the most authentic flavor if you can find a chile from Mesilla, New Mexico. These can be added to make the sauce mild or hot to your preference. These chiles have a mild to medium heat index and are marketed as Hatch or Anaheim chiles. Another option with the same heat index is the chipotle chile.

INGREDIENTS

20 stemmed **dried red chiles**, seeded (see note)

Several cloves **garlic**, peeled

½ **white onion**, peeled and cubed

Salt to taste

Guacamole

Historians note that guacamole was a dip or salad first created by the Aztecs. It has survived over the centuries to become one of the world's most popular Mexican dishes. It has become so popular that many supermarkets carry it ready-made. If you plan to make your own guacamole in advance of its use, place the avocado pits on top of the mixture to prevent it from turning brown, and refrigerate it.

Roughly mash the avocados with a potato masher. Add the scallions, chopped garlic, jalapeño, and fresh cilantro. Add the fresh lime juice, salt, and pepper to taste, mixing well. Place the avocado pits on top of the guacamole, cover with plastic wrap, and refrigerate until ready to serve.

INGREDIENTS
SERVES 4 TO 6

6 ripe **avocados**, preferably Haas, halved, pitted, and peeled

4 or 5 **scallions**, thinly sliced, white and light green parts only

5 cloves **garlic**, peeled and minced

1 **jalapeño pepper**, seeded and chopped, or to taste

6 to 8 sprigs fresh **cilantro**, finely chopped

Juice of 3 large **limes**

Salt and freshly ground **black pepper** to taste

Pastel de Tres Leches

Three-Milk Cake

Perhaps one of the most popular Latin desserts, this rich, moist cake has many variations, but the basics include the use of three types of milk: whole, evaporated, and sweetened condensed; hence the name "three milks," or *tres leches*. You may slice fresh strawberries and kiwis and place them on top of or on the sides of the cake, as you prefer. Note: Nestlé's La Lechera milk products are sold in the Latin food section of well-stocked supermarkets and in Latin grocery stores. Reserve any leftover sweetened condensed milk for another recipe.

1. Preheat the oven to 350 degrees. Use baking spray to prepare a deep-dish 9 x 13-inch baking pan. Set aside.

2. Sift together the flour, baking powder, and salt; set aside. Separate the eggs, placing the yolks in an electric blender or food processor, and the egg whites in a large bowl. Add ¾ cup sugar to the egg yolks, and blend on high for about 2 minutes or until the mixture is a pale yellow. Add ½ cup of milk and the vanilla, and mix briefly. In stages, add the dry ingredients and remaining milk, mixing in between to retain a smooth batter.

3. Using an electric mixer on high, beat the egg whites, gradually adding the remaining ¼ cup of sugar until they form stiff peaks.

4. Gently fold the batter by hand into the egg whites and mix, but do not overwork. Pour the mixture into the prepared pan.

5. Bake at 350 degrees for 25 minutes; then reduce the temperature to 300 degrees, and bake for another 10 minutes or until a wooden toothpick inserted in the center comes out clean. The cake will rise significantly. Remove from the oven, and allow the cake to cool completely. It will collapse to a thickness of about 2 inches.

6. Whip together the condensed milk, evaporated milk, whipping cream, and Grand Marnier or vanilla. Poke lots of holes all over the cake with a skewer or fork, and slowly pour the milk combination over the top and all around the edges. Cover the cake in plastic wrap, and refrigerate overnight to let the cake absorb the milk mixture.

7. For the topping, whip the cream and sugar together until stiff peaks form. Spread evenly over the surface of the cake. To serve, dust the surface of the cake with cinnamon, and decorate with fruit, if desired.

INGREDIENTS

SERVES 10 TO 12

FOR THE CAKE

1½ cups **all-purpose flour**

1 teaspoon **baking powder**

¼ teaspoon **salt**

4 large **eggs**, separated

1 cup **sugar**, divided

1½ cups **whole milk**

1 teaspoon **vanilla extract**

One 14-ounce can **sweetened condensed milk**

One 12-ounce can **evaporated milk**

¼ cup **whipping cream**

3 tablespoons **Grand Marnier** or 1 teaspoon **vanilla extract**

FOR THE TOPPING

2 cups **whipping cream**

3 tablespoons **sugar**

Ground **cinnamon** to taste

Fresh **strawberries** or **kiwis** (optional)

A Prayer to

OUR LADY OF GUADALUPE

Our Lady of Guadalupe, Mystical Rose,
make intercession for holy Church,
protect the sovereign pontiff,
help all those who invoke you in their necessities,
and since you are the ever Virgin Mary
and Mother of the true God,
obtain for us from your most holy Son
the grace of keeping our faith,
of sweet hope in the midst of the
bitterness of life, of burning charity, and the
precious gift of final perseverance. Amen.

DECEMBER 26

ST. STEPHEN

— Israel —

Born: circa 5, Died: circa 34

St. Stephen was one of the original deacons appointed by the apostles. When the Sanhedrin accused him of defaming Moses and declaring that Jesus would destroy the Temple, he defended Jesus and outlined all the mercies and graces God had bestowed on Israel.

Furious at these words, the witnesses threw St. Stephen out of town and began stoning him. As this was happening, he said: "Lord Jesus, receive my spirit.... Lord, do not hold this sin against them" (Acts 7:59-60). He died forgiving those who murdered him, just as Jesus had done. St. Stephen is remembered as the first Christian martyr.

ISRAELI BULGUR, WALNUT, AND FIG TABBOULEH

BULGUR IS DRIED CRACKED WHEAT and is available in different grinds, from fine to coarse, at Middle Eastern stores, well-stocked supermarkets, and online. For use in salads, such as this recipe, use fine-grain bulgur. Whole pomegranates are sold from September to January in well-stocked supermarkets. Online directions explain how to extract the seeds. But seeds sold separately are also available during these months and sold online as well.

Pomegranate molasses (or pomegranate syrup) is available at Middle Eastern stores as well as at some supermarkets. Before serving, let the salad rest for 20 minutes so the bulgur can absorb the flavors and become tender.

1. Preheat the oven to 350 degrees. Spread the walnut pieces on a baking sheet, and roast them for 5 minutes. Stir them, and return them to the oven for 5 minutes more. Remove, and place the sheet on a rack to cool completely.

2. Put the bulgur in a fine sieve or a fine-mesh colander, and wash it under running water for 60 seconds. Put it in a large bowl.

3. Make the dressing by mixing the olive oil, pomegranate molasses, red wine vinegar, honey, and salt to taste. Set aside.

4. When the walnuts are cool, put them in the food processor or blender, and pulse a few times until they resemble a rice grain. Add them to the bulgur. Add the figs and dressing, and mix; add the parsley, mint, scallions, and pomegranate seeds, and mix again. Set aside to rest for at least 20 minutes or until the bulgur is tender. Before serving, mix again, and adjust the seasonings.

INGREDIENTS
SERVES 6

1 cup **walnut pieces**

½ cup fine **bulgur**

¼ cup **olive oil**

2 tablespoons **pomegranate syrup**

1 tablespoon **red wine vinegar**

1 teaspoon **honey**

Kosher salt to taste

½ cup chopped **dried figs**

2 cups finely chopped **Italian parsley**

1 cup finely chopped **mint**

1 bunch **scallions**, thinly sliced

½ cup **pomegranate seeds**

DECEMBER 27

ST. JOHN
THE EVANGELIST

— *Israel* —

Born: 2 or 6, Died: 100

Known also as St. John the Beloved,
St. John the Apostle, and St. John the
Divine, this devout follower of Jesus
was the son of a Galilean fisherman
and the younger brother of St. James
the Great.

At the Crucifixion, being the only
apostle with Mary at the base of
the Cross, Jesus asked St. John to
become the guardian of Mary after
His death. After the Resurrection,
he apparently was the only apostle
to identify the risen Jesus at Lake
Tiberias.

St. John wrote the Gospel according
to John, as well as three epistles in
the New Testament and the book of
Revelation. He also baptized many
converts in Samaria and established
churches throughout Asia Minor.

ISRAELI ROASTED CHICKEN
in Pomegranate and Date Molasses

1. Combine the date molasses or syrup, olive oil, pomegranate molasses, and salt in a large ziplock bag. Use paper towels to pat the chicken dry, and add them to the bag. Seal it, pressing out as much air as possible. Massage to coat the chicken pieces evenly. Let them sit at room temperature for 30 minutes.

2. Preheat the oven to 425 degrees. Line a deep-dish baking pan with aluminum foil, and spray it with cooking oil.

3. Arrange the chicken in the baking pan with space between each piece. Pour the marinade evenly over the chicken. Roast for 5 minutes; then reduce the temperature to 400 degrees. Roast for 40 to 45 minutes, basting the chicken five or six times to keep it moist and glazed until the chicken is cooked through to an internal temperature of 170 degrees and its skin is crisp and browned. Remove from the oven, and let the chicken rest for 5 minutes before serving.

INGREDIENTS
SERVES 6

½ cup **date molasses** or **syrup** (see the recipe on the following page)

⅓ cup **olive oil**

¼ cup **pomegranate molasses** (see note)

2 teaspoons **kosher salt**

6 **chicken legs with thighs attached**, about 4 pounds total

Pomegranate molasses (or pomegranate syrup) is available at Middle Eastern stores and well-stocked supermarkets.

DATE MOLASSES

Date molasses is a healthy sweetener that is used in many Middle Eastern recipes. Adjust the quantity of dates and water used for the amount you want to end up with. Like honey and other molasses, it does not need to be refrigerated and won't spoil.

INGREDIENTS

Pitted dates

Water

1. Place your desired amount of pitted dates into a saucepan, and cover with water about ¼ to ½ inch above the dates.

2. Bring to a boil, and cook about 10 minutes or until the dates are very soft and plump.

3. Remove the mixture from the heat, and let cool for about 3 minutes.

4. Transfer the mixture to a food processor or blender, and purée until a thick syrup forms. Store any unused molasses in a plastic container with a lid.

CELEBRATORY COOKIES

THE HISTORY *of* CELEBRATORY COOKIES

It may come as a surprise to many of today's cooks that sweet and spicy baked goods date back centuries before Christ.

By the Middle Ages cultural rituals had changed. Celebrating special Church holidays surpassed any solstice observations. By then, spices, sugar, lard, butter, and dried fruits were more readily available, and cooks began creating and baking festive baked goods. Historians note that Queen Elizabeth I was the first monarch to eat a shaped gingerbread cookie.

By the sixteenth century, Scandinavian, German, and Dutch bakers were busily assembling their own festive biscuits and other baked goods. In 1796, the first American cookbook, *American Cookery* by Amelia Simmons, was published. It featured a holiday cookie called a "Christmas Cookey," described as dry and hard and requiring extensive aging. Today's cooks have access to thousands of tempting cookies and baked goods that are decorated, shaped, frosted, glazed, or topped with candies.

Cooks from many cultures have developed artistic and delicious offerings to celebrate and honor their favorite saints.

FEAST DAY COOKIE INDEX

JANUARY 21

ST. AGNES

ST. AGNES COOKIES

MAKES ABOUT 5 DOZEN 1¾-INCH SANDWICH COOKIES

FROM AN OLD GERMAN FAMILY RECIPE, these cookies are a labor of love because they take time to put together. They are sweet even without the chocolate cover, but the chocolate-and-nut topping enhance their eye appeal. First-timers may want to start with half the recipe, unless these will be a treat for a large family. The following recipe is separated into three parts: the dough, the filling, and the decoration.

FOR THE DOUGH

1. Combine the butter and sugar in a large mixing bowl, and using an electric mixer on medium speed, beat the mixture until creamy. Add the vanilla and lemon zest. Sift together the flour, baking soda, and baking powder in a separate bowl. Slowly fold the flour into the butter mixture. When the dough looks flaky, turn it onto a work surface dusted with flour. Knead the dough by hand for 5 to 7 minutes or until it is smooth. Refrigerate the dough for at least 1 hour.

2. Preheat the oven to 325 degrees. Line baking sheets with parchment paper, and set aside.

3. Roll out the dough on a work surface dusted with flour until it is ⅛ inch thick. Use a round cookie cutter with scalloped edges or any other simple cookie cutter. Place the cookie cutouts on the baking sheets.

4. Bake for 8 to 10 minutes or until golden. Move the cookies onto cooling racks, and cool them completely.

FOR THE FILLING

To make the filling, dust two sheets of foil with confectioners' sugar, place the marzipan between the sheets, and roll it out until very thin. Use the same cookie cutter to cut out marzipan shapes. Brush the undersides of two cookies thinly with jam, and layer the marzipan cutout between the two cookies. Repeat until all the cookies are assembled.

DOUGH INGREDIENTS

1 cup (8 ounces) **unsalted butter**

1 cup **sugar**

1 teaspoon **vanilla extract**

Zest of 1 **lemon**

2¼ cups **all-purpose flour**

1 teaspoon **baking soda**

½ teaspoon **baking powder**

FILLING INGREDIENTS

12 ounces **marzipan**

Confectioners' sugar for rolling out marzipan

6 tablespoons **seedless jam** of your choice

FOR THE DECORATION

To decorate the cookies, if desired, brush one side of each cookie with a thin coat of melted chocolate, and sprinkle the top with chopped nuts. Alternately, dust them with confectioners' sugar.

DECORATION INGREDIENTS
(OPTIONAL)

8 ounces **semisweet chocolate chips**, melted

½ cup **walnut pieces**, chopped

½ cup **slivered almonds**

½ cup **pistachio nuts**, chopped

Confectioners' sugar for dusting

FEBRUARY 2

THE PURIFICATION
OF OUR LADY

NAVETTES

MAKES ABOUT 7 DOZEN 1½-INCH-LONG COOKIES OR 3½ DOZEN 3-INCH-LONG COOKIES

In the French city of Marseille, bakers have developed a special cookie to celebrate Our Lady's feast day and to commemorate her arrival in France with St. Mary Magdalene; her sister, St. Martha; and her brother, St. Lazarus. To honor Our Lady's arrival by boat, the bakers shaped their cookies to resemble little boats—hence, the name *navettes*, which means "little boats" in French. The original recipe has been kept a secret since 1781 by some of the oldest bakeries in Marseille. Traditionally, navettes are consumed when they are cold. The French dip them in coffee, tea, or wine.

1. Combine the flour, sugar, and salt in a large bowl, and using an electric mixer on medium speed, beat together until well blended. Stir in the lemon zest. In a second bowl, whisk the eggs and olive oil together. Stir in the orange blossom water and the vanilla by hand. Pour the egg mixture over the flour mixture, and mix quickly, first with a wooden spoon and, as the mix becomes flaky, by hand. Turn the dough onto a clean work surface, and knead firmly by hand for 5 to 7 minutes or until it is smooth. Let the dough rest for 15 minutes.

2. Preheat the oven to 350 degrees. Line 2 baking sheets with parchment paper. Set aside.

3. Form the dough into rolls about ¾ inch thick. Cut off pieces about 1½ inches long. Pinch both ends with your index finger and thumb, and use a knife to make a lengthwise incision in the middle. This should give the cookies the appearance of little boats. Place on the prepared baking sheets about ½ inch apart. Brush with the milk, if desired.

4. Bake until the cookies are golden brown on the underside, about 15 minutes. The 3-inch-long cookies should bake for about 25 minutes. Remove from the oven, and cool completely on a rack.

INGREDIENTS

2¼ cups **all-purpose flour**

1 cup **sugar**

Pinch **salt**

Zest of 1 **lemon**

2 large **eggs**

⅓ cup **olive oil**

3 tablespoons **orange blossom water**

1 teaspoon **vanilla extract**

Milk for brushing (optional)

MARCH 17

ST. PATRICK

ST. PATRICK'S DAY
PISTACHIO COOKIES

MAKES 3½ DOZEN COOKIES

THESE GREEN COOKIES HONOR ST. PATRICK on his feast day, when green is the go-to color. Note: Some recipes instruct that you use a pestle to crush the nuts, but you will get a finer texture by grinding the pistachios in a blender or food processor. Adding ground cinnamon to the applesauce intensifies the spiciness.

1. Preheat the oven to 300 degrees. Line 3 baking sheets with parchment paper. Set aside.

2. Combine the avocado and butter in the container of a blender or food processor, and process until creamy and smooth. Add the applesauce, sugar, and milk, and process to combine. Add the egg and vanilla extract, and process to combine. Add the pudding mix, baking powder, and salt, and process again. Fold in the ground nuts and the flour, and stir to blend well. Place heaping teaspoonfuls of dough on the baking sheets.

3. Bake the cookies for about 20 minutes. Watch closely, and remove from the oven when the bottoms of the cookies begin to brown. Let them rest on the baking sheets for 5 to 10 minutes before moving them to a cooling rack.

INGREDIENTS

½ ripe fresh **avocado**, peeled and pit removed

¼ cup (4 ounces) **unsalted butter**, softened

½ cup **applesauce** with ¼ teaspoon **cinnamon**, ground

½ cup **sugar**

¼ cup **whole milk**

1 large **egg**

1 teaspoon **vanilla extract**

Two 3.4-ounce packages **instant pistachio pudding mix**

1 teaspoon **baking powder**

¼ teaspoon **salt**

⅔ cup unsalted **pistachios**, peeled and ground

1 cup **all-purpose flour**

APRIL 11

ST. STANISLAUS
OF KRAKÓW

KOLACZKI
Polish Filled Cookies

MAKES ABOUT 5 TO 6 DOZEN COOKIES

IN 1072, ST. STANISLAUS BECAME THE BISHOP OF KRAKÓW, Poland. The saint was an advocate for the peasantry against the evil dictates of King Boleslaus II. Despite death threats against him, St. Stanislaus also excommunicated the king. The angry king demanded that his soldiers murder the saint, and when they refused, the king himself killed St. Stanislaus.

1. Combine the butter and cream cheese in a mixing bowl, and using an electric mixer on medium speed, beat them together until light and fluffy. Stir in the flour and salt. Wrap the dough in plastic wrap, and chill for 1 hour.

2. Meanwhile, to make the filling, pour 1½ cups of water into a saucepan, and add the dried apricots and sugar. Heat over medium heat, and cook until the apricots become tender, about 15 minutes. Using a blender, purée the mixture, and set aside.

3. Preheat the oven to 350 degrees. Line a baking sheet with parchment paper, and set aside.

4. Dust a work surface with a sprinkling of granulated sugar. Roll out the dough to ¼ inch thick. Cut it into 2-inch squares. Place a teaspoon of filling in the center of each square. Fold over the opposite corners, and seal well. Place on the cookie sheet.

5. Bake for 15 minutes or until the corners start to turn golden. Remove from the heat. Set aside to cool. When the cookies are completely cooled, dust them with confectioners' sugar.

PASTRY INGREDIENTS

1 ½ cups (12 ounces) **unsalted butter**, at room temperature

8 ounces **cream cheese**, at room temperature

3 cups **all-purpose flour**

½ teaspoon **salt**

Granulated sugar for dusting surface

Confectioners' sugar for dusting cookies

FILLING INGREDIENTS

¾ cup **dried apricots** or other dried fruit

2 tablespoons **sugar**

1 teaspoon **lemon juice**

MAY 15

ST. ISIDORE THE
FARMER

ROSQUILLAS DE SAN ISIDRO

St. Isidore Shortbread Cookies

MAKES 7 DOZEN COOKIES

To honor the patron saint of Madrid, St. Isidore the Farmer, the people of the city gather to celebrate his special day with these traditional shortbread cookies, which are less sweet than the typical American version. For a sweeter cookie, add more sugar.

1. Heat the olive oil in a large saucepan over medium heat; do not let the oil come to a boil. Add the lemon rind in large pieces. Reduce the heat to low, and cook for 12 to 15 minutes or until the skin pieces turn crispy and brown. Remove the rind, and let the oil cool. Line baking sheets with parchment paper, and set aside.

2. In a separate bowl, using an electric mixer on medium speed, combine the sugar and the eggs. Stir the flour into the mixture in small batches until well combined. Stir in the ground anise seeds. Slowly add the cooled oil, forming a smooth dough. Transfer the dough to a floured work surface, and knead by hand for 7 minutes. Pinch off walnut-size pieces of dough, roll them into finger-thick pieces about 4 inches long, and form them into doughnuts. Smooth the connection of the ends, and place the doughnuts on the baking sheets at least 1 inch apart. Spray or brush them with olive oil. Let the dough rest for 1 hour.

3. Preheat the oven to 375 degrees. Bake the cookies for 10 to 12 minutes, remove from the oven, and cool completely.

4. Meanwhile, prepare the glaze. Mix the confectioners' sugar with the lemon juice. If it is too thin and runny, add more sugar. If it is too thick, sparingly add a little water at a time, and mix well. Brush onto the cooled cookies, and let dry. If desired, you can add a few drops of food coloring to the glaze.

INGREDIENTS

THE COOKIES

½ cup **olive oil** plus extra

Rind of 1 **lemon** in large strips without pith

1 tablespoon **anise seeds**, finely ground with mortar and pestle

½ cup **sugar**, or more to taste

4 large **eggs**

2 ½ cups **all-purpose flour**

THE GLAZE

1 cup **confectioners' sugar**

2 to 3 tablespoons **lemon juice**

JUNE 21

ST. TERENCE

SEKERPARE
Turkish Semolina Cookies
MAKES 20 3-INCH COOKIES

St. Terence lived in the first century and officiated as the first bishop of Iconium, in present-day Turkey. Church historians believe that he may be the man called Tertius mentioned by St. Paul in his Letter to the Romans. St. Terence apparently, at St. Paul's dictation, wrote the Letter to the Romans.

The word *sekerpare* means "a piece of sweet" in the ancient Turkish language. Even to this day, this beloved Turkish dessert is enjoyed and often accompanies Turkish coffee or tea.

1. Preheat the oven to 350 degrees. Line baking sheets with parchment paper, and set aside.

2. Grate the lemon zest, and set aside. To make the syrup, squeeze the lemon juice into a cup, and set aside. Combine 2 cups of water and the sugar in a heavy saucepan, and bring to a boil over medium heat. Stir and let the sugar dissolve. Add the lemon juice, reduce the heat to low, and cook for 15 minutes more, until the syrup thickens slightly. Remove from the heat, and set the syrup aside to cool.

3. To make the dough, melt the butter in a saucepan over low heat or in the microwave. Sift the flour into a large mixing bowl, and stir in the semolina. Make a well in the center, and pour in the butter. Stir in the eggs, sugar, olive oil, baking powder, and lemon zest. On a lightly floured surface, knead the dough for 5 minutes, until it is soft and moist. Cover with a damp cloth, and set aside to rest for 15 minutes.

4. Knead the dough again for 5 minutes. Wet your hands lightly with cold water, divide the dough, and shape into 20 ping pong–size balls. Place the sekerpare dough balls side by side, making sure to leave at least 1 1/2 inches of space between them. Gently press down on top of each ball to flatten it slightly. Push an almond or hazelnut into the center of each sekerpare ball.

INGREDIENTS

THE SYRUP

2 cups water

Juice of 1 **lemon**

1 1/2 cups **sugar**

THE DOUGH

1/2 cup plus 1 tablespoon **unsalted butter**

2 cups **all-purpose flour**

1/2 cup fine **semolina**

2 large **eggs**, lightly beaten

1/2 cup **sugar**

2 tablespoons light **olive oil**

1 tablespoon **baking powder**

Zest of 1 **lemon**

20 blanched **almonds** or **hazelnuts**

5. Bake for 20 to 25 minutes or until the cookies turn light brown. Remove the cookies from the oven, and pour the cooled syrup over them immediately. Set them aside to cool and to soak up the syrup for 15 minutes; the sekerpare will get soft and tender. Store them in a covered container at room temperature for 2 to 3 days.

JULY 22

ST. MARY
MAGDALENE

FRENCH MADELEINES

MAKES ABOUT 6 DOZEN 3¼ x 2-INCH COOKIES

THERE ARE MANY OPINIONS ON WHO OR WHAT gave the unofficial national cookie of France its name; none of them, however, can claim to have existed before the arrival of Mary Magdalene in the company of Our Lady on France's shores. *Madeleine* is the French version of the name Magdalene.

The trick to giving these cookies their traditional "bump" is to use eggs at room temperature. Cooks must be very gentle when preparing the batter, taking care not to overwork it. That way, it cannot deflate before or after baking. Cool the baked cookies on wire cooling racks until cold, as they will stick to any other surface. Madeleine cookie molds are readily available where bakeware is sold. Alternatively, cooks may use mini muffin tins.

1. Combine the eggs and the sugar in a mixing bowl, and beat them together at medium speed until fluffy and very pale; this may take several minutes. Reduce the speed to the lowest setting, and slowly add the butter, yogurt, and honey. Stir in the orange blossom water, vanilla extract, and lemon zest by hand, and mix well. Do not overwork the batter. It needs to remain fluffy and airy.

2. In a separate bowl, mix together the flour, ground almonds, baking powder, and salt. Fold the dry ingredients in small batches into the egg mixture by hand. Using a rubber spatula, gently fold the batter over the flour mix; do not overbeat. Chill for 30 minutes.

3. Preheat the oven to 350 degrees. Spray the molds evenly with baking spray. Fill the molds ⅔ full with the batter.

4. Bake for 10 to 12 minutes. Remove from the oven, and cool the molds on cooling racks. Once the cookies are cool enough to slip out of the molds, place them directly on the cooling racks to cool completely.

INGREDIENTS

5 large **eggs**, at room temperature

⅓ cup **sugar**

1 cup (8 ounces) very soft **unsalted butter**

½ cup natural **plain** or **Greek yogurt**

½ cup **honey**

2 tablespoons **orange blossom water**, or more as desired, or 1 teaspoon **orange essence**

1 teaspoon **vanilla extract**

Zest of 1 **lemon**

1 ½ cups **all-purpose flour**, sifted

½ cup **almonds**, peeled and finely ground

1 teaspoon **baking powder**

½ teaspoon **salt**

Note: If you'd like to coat one side of the Madeleines with chocolate, melt chocolate in a water bath, brush a thin layer into the previously used (silicone or greased again) molds, and immediately insert the Madeleines again. Let cool naturally or chill in the refrigerator. When completely cold, remove from the mold.

AUGUST 3
ST. LYDIA
PURPURARIA

GREEK LAVENDER COOKIES

MAKES 7 DOZEN COOKIES

THESE LAVENDER-FLAVORED COOKIES honor St. Lydia Purpuraria ("purple dye"), who was a vendor of purple dye in Greece. She was St. Paul's first convert in Philippi.

1. Combine the sugar and butter in a large mixing bowl. Cream together the sugar and butter, and using an electric mixer on medium speed, beat until light and fluffy. Add the eggs one at a time, beating well after each addition. Stir in the vanilla and almond extracts.

2. In a separate bowl, stir together the flour, almond flour, lavender flowers, baking powder, and salt. Gently fold the flour mixture into the butter mixture. Refrigerate for at least 1 hour.

3. Preheat the oven to 350 degrees. Line 2 baking sheets with parchment paper. Set aside.

4. Drop rounded teaspoonfuls of dough onto the baking sheets 2 inches apart. Bake for 12 minutes or until golden. Let cool on the baking sheets for 3 minutes before removing to a cooling rack.

Note: You will need about 3½ tablespoons whole lavender flowers (organic, food grade) before grinding them.

INGREDIENTS

1 ¼ cups **sugar**

1 cup (8 ounces) **unsalted butter**

2 jumbo **eggs**

1 teaspoon **vanilla extract**

½ teaspoon **almond extract**

2 ¼ cups **all-purpose flour**

¼ cup very finely ground **almond flour**

2 tablespoons finely ground dried **lavender flowers** (see note)

1 ½ teaspoons **baking powder**

½ teaspoon **salt**

AUGUST 11

ST. CLARE

TORTITAS DE SANTA CLARA
Santa Clara Cookies

MAKES ABOUT 2 DOZEN 3-INCH COOKIES

A POPULAR MEXICAN COOKIE relatively unknown elsewhere, these sweets were likely created by the nuns in the Santa Clara convent in Puebla during Mexico's colonial period. Although they resemble a classic shortbread, what makes them unusual is that they are topped with a native Mexican ingredient: pumpkin seeds. Making these cookies is time-consuming because the pumpkin seeds need to be soaked and hulled. For a faster result, use almonds when making the glaze.

FOR THE COOKIE

1. Put the butter into a mixer, and beat it on medium speed until creamy. Reduce the speed to the lowest setting, and gently fold in the confectioners' sugar and baking powder. Continue mixing until everything is incorporated.

2. Add the flour, 1 cup at a time, and then the egg yolks, one at a time; continue beating for a minute. Pour in the water, and continue mixing until the dough is smooth and can form a ball. Wrap the dough in plastic wrap, and place it in the refrigerator. Let it cool until it hardens enough to be manageable, for at least 30 minutes or up to several days.

3. When ready to bake, preheat the oven to 375 degrees, and cover a baking sheet with parchment paper. Set aside.

4. Place half the dough on a piece of lightly floured parchment paper, sprinkle flour over it, and place another piece of parchment paper on top. Using a rolling pin, gently roll out the dough to about ¼ inch thick. Remove the top piece of parchment paper, and using a 3-inch cookie cutter, cut out circles.

COOKIE INGREDIENTS

½ cup **unsalted butter**, at room temperature

1 cup **confectioners' sugar**

¼ teaspoon **baking powder**

3 cups **all-purpose flour** plus more for rolling out dough

3 **egg yolks**

½ cup lukewarm **water**

5. Using a smaller cookie cutter, make a circular indention in the middle of each cookie without cutting all the way through the dough; leave about ¼ inch space between the indentation and the edge. Press the edges of each cookie with a fork to give them a pretty pattern. Repeat the process with the remaining dough. Space the cookies at least ¼ inch apart on the baking sheet.

6. Bake for about 10 minutes or until the cookies are fully cooked and the bottoms are lightly browned. Remove them from the oven, and let cool; repeat with the remaining cookies.

7. Once the cookies have cooled, add about 1 tablespoon of glaze to each cookie.

THE GLAZE

Note: The white candied pumkin seed glaze, as traditionally made by the nuns of the Santa Clara convent, achieves its color through a more time-consuming seed preparation process. For a less laborious glaze, you may make a green glaze by placing hulled, unsalted pumpkin seeds into a blender or food processor and grinding them completely, or you may make an easier white glaze by placing blanched, slivered almonds into a blender or food processor and grinding them completely.

First, prepare the pumpkin seeds:

1. Bring water to a boil in a small saucepan, add the pumpkin seeds, simmer for about 5 minutes, and turn off the heat. Let it cool, stir in the baking soda or baking powder, and let it sit overnight.

2. With your hands, rub the pumpkin seeds between your fingers and thumbs to release their skins. The skins will float in the water. Carefully pour off the water, cover again with clean water, and drain again. With a slotted spatula, place the pumpkin seeds on a clean kitchen towel, rubbing them so that the remaining skins come entirely off.

3. Place the seeds in a bowl, cover them with water, rinse, and place them on a cloth towel or paper towels to dry.

GLAZE INGREDIENTS

2 cups **sugar**

½ cup **water**

3 cups raw, hulled **pumpkin seeds** or slivered **almonds**

½ cup **whole milk**

TO BLANCH THE PUMPKIN SEEDS

½ teaspoon **baking powder** or **baking soda**

After the pumpkin seeds have been prepared, prepare the glaze:

4.   Place the sugar and ¼ cup of water in a medium saucepan over medium-low heat. Cook until the sugar has completely dissolved, is no longer granulated, and appears to be a light syrup, about 8 to 10 minutes. Add the ground pumpkin seeds or almonds, and stir well, creating a thick paste. Let the mixture cook for another 3 to 4 minutes. It will thicken and become even more pasty. Turn off the heat, pour in the milk, and stir well. It should be thick yet shiny and a bit more liquid.

5.   Remove the mixture from the heat, and let it cool until it slightly thickens and can top the cookie without spilling over. It will spread as it settles, but if it has cooled enough, it will not be too runny. If the mixture hardens, just reheat it over low heat with a tablespoon of water until it becomes soft again.

AUGUST 18

ST. HELENA

HELENENSCHNITTEN MIT MARZIPAN

St. Helena Cookies with Marzipan

MAKES ABOUT 5 DOZEN COOKIES

An empress of the Roman Empire and the mother of Constantine the Great, eighty-year-old St. Helena marched with part of her son's army to the Holy Land. There she discovered the relics of the True Cross.

1. Preheat the oven to 350 degrees. Line a 1½-inch-deep, approximately 14x15-inch baking sheet with parchment paper, and set aside.

2. Combine the flour, butter, eggs, egg yolks, confectioners' sugar, ground almonds, ground chocolate, and vanilla extract in a large bowl. Fold and mix them together to form a smooth dough. If the dough seems too sticky, add more flour, up to ½ cup. Cover the dough, and chill it for 2 to 3 hours.

3. Prepare the filling by whipping together the marzipan and egg whites on medium speed until the mixture is lump free.

4. Next, split the dough into two equal parts. Roll out each half to fit the size of your baking sheet. Place one half on the prepared baking sheet. Spread the marzipan mixture over the entire surface. Cover with the other half of the dough. Gently press down and poke with a fork several times to keep air bubbles from forming.

5. Bake for 15 to 20 minutes. Remove from the oven, and cool on the baking sheet.

6. Prepare the glaze by whipping together the confectioners' sugar, rum, water, and cinnamon on medium speed until well combined.

7. Brush the top of the cooked dough with the glaze, and let it dry. Cut strips about 1 inch wide and 3 inches long from the dried cookie. If stored in a metal tin, the cookies can last 3 to 4 weeks.

INGREDIENTS

FOR THE DOUGH

4 cups **all-purpose flour**

1 ¼ cups (10 ounces) cold **unsalted butter**

3 large **eggs**

3 **egg yolks**

2 cups **confectioners' sugar**

1 cup finely ground **almonds**

1 cup finely ground **semisweet chocolate**

2 teaspoons **vanilla extract**

FOR THE FILLING

10½ ounces **marzipan**

3 **egg whites**

FOR THE GLAZE

2 cups **confectioners' sugar**

3 tablespoons **rum**

3 tablespoons **water**

1 teaspoon ground **cinnamon**

SEPTEMBER 2

ST. INGRID OF SWEDEN

VANILJKAKORS
Swedish Vanilla Cookies

MAKES 2½ DOZEN COOKIES

Sᴛ. Iɴɢʀɪᴅ, who lived in the thirteenth century, was the first Dominican nun in Sweden.

1. Preheat the oven to 350 degrees. Line 2 baking sheets with parchment paper, and set aside.

2. Using an electric mixer on medium speed, cream the butter and sugar until well mixed. Scrape down the sides and bottom of the bowl, beat again, and cream until light and fluffy. Beat in the egg yolk and vanilla extract. Scrape down the sides of the bowl, and beat in the flour. Blend thoroughly.

3. Roll the dough into walnut-size balls, and place them on the baking sheet. Using the handle of a wooden spoon, make an indentation on the top of each cookie. Scoop some jam or preserves into each indentation.

4. Bake for about 15 minutes or until pale golden. Remove the sheet from the oven, and set aside to cool. Dust the cookies with confectioners' sugar. Store them in an airtight container.

INGREDIENTS

1 cup (8 ounces) **unsalted butter**, softened

⅔ cup **confectioners' sugar** plus extra for dusting

1 extra-large **egg yolk**

1 tablespoon **vanilla extract**

2 ¼ cups sifted **all-purpose flour** (see note)

⅓ cup **jam** or **preserves** of your choice

Sift the flour first before measuring it in the cup. Then level the top with a knife or spatula.

OCTOBER 2
GUARDIAN ANGELS

ANGEL WINGS

MAKES ABOUT 3 DOZEN COOKIES

THESE TRADITIONAL COOKIES shaped like wings are popular in several countries and have many names. This recipe is not to be confused with the Polish Angel Wing cookies called *chrusciki* or the Russia *khrystiki*. It offers a different wing shape with cinnamon sprinkled in the wing's curves. These are enjoyed during holidays and special celebrations, such as weddings.

1. Place the flour in a large mixing bowl. Cut the butter into the flour until the mixture resembles coarse crumbs. Stir in the sour cream.

2. Turn the dough onto a lightly floured work surface. Knead the dough 6 to 8 times or until the mixture holds together. Shape the dough into 4 balls, and flatten them slightly. Wrap the dough in plastic wrap, and refrigerate it for 4 hours or overnight.

3. After refrigerating, unwrap one ball of dough. Lay out a sheet of wax paper, and sprinkle 2 tablespoons of sugar on it. Coat all sides of the dough ball with sugar. Place a second sheet of wax paper on top of the dough, and roll the dough into a 12x15-inch rectangle. Remove the top sheet of wax paper, and lightly sprinkle the surface with ¾ teaspoon cinnamon. Lightly mark a line down the center of the dough, marking two 6x5-inch rectangles.

4. Starting with the shorter (5-inch) side, roll the dough, jellyroll style, toward the marked center line, peeling the waxed paper away while rolling. Repeat, coming from the other 5-inch side, so the two rolls meet in the center. Wrap in plastic wrap, and freeze for 30 minutes. Repeat this with the other three balls of dough.

5. Preheat the oven to 375 degrees. Place the remaining sugar or the colored sugar on wax paper. Remove one roll from the freezer, and unwrap it. Cut it into ½-inch-thick slices, and dip each side into the sugar. Place the slices 2 inches apart on ungreased baking sheets.

6. Bake for 13 minutes or until golden brown. Turn the cookies over, and bake for 5 to 8 minutes longer. Remove the cookies from the oven, and place the sheets on wire racks to cool.

INGREDIENTS

1 ½ cups **all-purpose flour**

1 cup (8 ounces) cold **butter**, cubed

½ cup **sour cream**

10 tablespoons **sugar**, divided

3 teaspoons ground **cinnamon**, divided

Colored **sugar** (optional)

OCTOBER 4

ST. FRANCIS OF ASSISI

I MOSTACCIOLI DEL SAN FRANCESCO D'ASSISI

St. Francis of Assisi Cookies

MAKES ABOUT 10 DOZEN 1¼ x 2¼-INCH COOKIES

A ROMAN NOBLEWOMAN named Jacopa dei Settesoli, a supporter of St. Francis, brought the saint her version of this cookie as he lay on his deathbed. He enjoyed them with great love, so the story goes. These sweet, nut-filled treats make a delicious dessert accompaniment.

1. Preheat the oven to 300 degrees. Line 3 or 4 baking sheets with parchment paper, and set aside.

2. In a large bowl, combine all the ingredients, and work them into a dough. Refrigerate the dough for at least 30 minutes or overnight, to let it become firm.

3. Slice off part of the dough and roll it out to ⅛ inch thick. Using a sharp knife, cut long, narrow strips about 1¼ inches wide. Using the knife at an angle, cut off 2¼-inch diamonds from each strip. Place on the prepared baking sheets, leaving about ¼ inch between each cookie.

4. Bake for 15 minutes or until done. Remove from the oven, and place the sheets on cooling racks.

INGREDIENTS

1 cup **almonds**, peeled and ground

¾ cup **hazelnuts**, peeled and ground

2 cups **all-purpose flour**

2 teaspoons **cinnamon**, ground (see note)

1½ cups **sugar**

¾ cup **honey**

4 tablespoons lukewarm **water**

For enhanced spiciness, grind your own cinnamon stick.

NOVEMBER 16

ST. MARGARET
OF SCOTLAND

SCOTTISH SHORTBREAD COOKIES

MAKES 6 DOZEN 1½-INCH COOKIES

1. Preheat the oven to 325 degrees. Line 2 or 3 baking sheets with parchment paper, and set aside.

2. Place all the ingredients in a large mixing bowl. Using an electric mixer on medium speed, blend them together until well combined into a dough.

3. Flour a work surface, and roll the dough out to about ¼ inch thick. Using a pizza slicer or a knife, cut the dough into 1½-inch-square pieces or any other preferable shape. Place the pieces on the baking sheet. Pierce the top of each cookie twice with a fork.

4. Bake for 20 minutes or until golden. Remove from the oven, and set aside to cool completely on wire racks.

INGREDIENTS

2 cups **all-purpose flour**

1 cup (8 ounces) **unsalted butter**, softened

½ cup firmly packed **brown sugar**

¼ teaspoon **salt**

NOVEMBER 25

ST. CATHERINE OF ALEXANDRIA

THORNER KATHRINCHEN
St. Catherine Cookies

MAKES ABOUT 7 DOZEN 2-INCH COOKIES

THE EARLIEST MENTION of a recipe for these sweets dates back to 1293. They were created in a monastery kitchen in Schleinitz, Germany. Years later, the recipe became public in Nuremberg and Munich. Traditionally, the dough had to rest for seven to fourteen days so the full aroma of the spices had time to develop. Because St. Catherine's feast day is on November 25, preparing the cookie dough became an overture to the season of Advent.

FOR THE DOUGH

1. In a medium saucepan, heat the honey with the sugar and butter. Stir to combine. Remove from the heat, and let cool.

2. Using an electric mixer on medium speed, beat the eggs with the spices until well combined. Add the almond extract and lemon juice. Mix in the honey mixture, and beat until well combined.

3. Sift the flour with the baking soda in a separate bowl, and mix well. Add this mixture to the honey and spice mix in small batches. If the dough becomes too stiff, add rum or water. Knead until firm but smooth. Place the dough in a bowl, cover the dough, and refrigerate it overnight.

4. When ready to bake, preheat the oven to 325 degrees. Line baking sheets with parchment paper, and set aside. Roll out the dough to ¼ inch thick, and cut out the cookies with a round cutter. Place them on the sheets.

5. Bake for 10 to 15 minutes or until firm. Remove from the oven, and set aside to cool completely.

FOR THE GLAZE

Combine the lemon juice with the confectioners' sugar. If it is too thick, add a few drops of water to thin it. If it is too thin, add more sugar. Brush each cookie with glaze.

INGREDIENTS

THE DOUGH

2 cups **honey**

1 ½ cups **sugar**

½ cup (4 ounces) **unsalted butter**

1 ½ cups **almonds**, blanched and finely ground

2 large **eggs**

2 teaspoons **cinnamon**, ground

1 teaspoon **cloves**, ground

1 teaspoon **cardamom**, ground

1 teaspoon **ginger**, ground

1 teaspoon **nutmeg**, ground

Pinch **salt**

3 drops **almond extract**

Zest of 1 **orange**

3 cups **all-purpose flour**

1 ½ teaspoons **baking soda**

2 tablespoons **lemon juice**

¼ cup **rum** or **water**, optional

FOR THE GLAZE

Juice of 1 **lemon**

1 cup **confectioners' sugar**

Few drops **water**, if needed

DECEMBER 6

ST. NICHOLAS

ST. NIKOLAAS KOEKJES
St. Nicholas Cookies

MAKES 3 TO 4 DOZEN COOKIES

MANY CULTURES HAVE DELICIOUS VERSIONS of what has become a holiday spice cookie to celebrate St. Nicholas. Often the cookies are cut out in the shape of St. Nicholas or in other liturgical shapes with specials cutters. Although this recipe does not call for it, baked and cooled cookies could be iced in holiday décor with festive sprinkles. Note: For those with dietary issues, use a cholesterol-free product instead of butter and certain Greek yogurts that are almost cholesterol free.

1. Stir together the flour, baking soda, salt, cinnamon, nutmeg, and cloves in a mixing bowl. In another bowl, with a mixer, cream the butter and sugar until well blended. Stir in the sour cream until smooth. Gradually add the flour mixture, and beat gently to form a dough. Fold in the nuts. Transfer the dough onto wax paper, and shape it into a log with a diameter of 2 inches. Wrap the dough in wax paper or plastic wrap, and refrigerate for at least 8 hours or overnight.

2. When ready to bake, preheat the oven to 350 degrees. Line baking sheets with parchment paper, and set aside.

3. After refrigerating the dough, firm it up in the freezer for about 30 minutes for easier slicing. Slice the log into pieces about ¼ inch thick. Place the pieces 1 inch apart on the baking sheet.

4. Bake for 8 to 10 minutes or until golden brown. Remove from the oven, and transfer the cookies to a wire rack. Allow the cookies to cool until crispy.

INGREDIENTS

2 cups **all-purpose flour**

¼ teaspoon **baking soda**

Pinch **salt**

2 teaspoons **cinnamon**, ground

¼ teaspoon **nutmeg**, ground

¼ teaspoon **cloves**, ground

1 cup (8 ounces) **unsalted butter**, at room temperature

1 cup **sugar**

¼ cup **sour cream**

¼ to ½ cup chopped **walnuts**

Reflections on Food and Faith

In the beginning . . .

From the very beginning of the world, food and faith have been interwoven by the creative and loving hand of God, making food the meeting point between this world and the heavenly kingdom. Not only did God intentionally create us in such a way that food was required to sustain natural bodily life, but He also made food the avenue by which we would receive the gift of supernatural life. In paradise God planted fruit trees, the Tree of Life and the Tree of Knowledge of Good and Evil. From the Tree of Life, Adam and Eve were to receive the gift of Eternal life—God's life. But from the Tree of Knowledge of Good and Evil man was not to eat, lest, through disobedience, he discover life apart from God—death. We might say that with the creation of the Tree of Life, God invited man to the first great feast. And with the creation of the Tree of Knowledge, God introduced man to the first great fast. In his *Hymns on Paradise*, St. Ephrem the Syrian explains that the Tree of Knowledge, and the fast that God set around it, was the gateway through which Adam and Eve were to walk so as to discover the banquet of God. From this first encounter with food in the book of Genesis, we discover something important about God's plan for us: that through food and faith-filled self-control, we were meant to find the path that leads to eternal life.

We can say, then, that food is meant to be the bearer of the life of the one who gives it. When food is prepared as a gift by one who loves, the one who receives the gift receives more than food: he receives the food charged with love, charged with the life of the one who lovingly prepares it. And when one gives in love and one receives in love, the original plan of God for the communion of His people is restored.

—Fr. Hezekias (Sabatino) Carnazzo
Founding Executive Director, Institute of Catholic Culture,
Pastor, St. George Melkite Greek-Catholic Church,
Sacramento, California

Cooking with the Saints is the fruit (no pun intended) of nearly ten years of cooking classes at our parish. Each class focused on a specific country's food. In addition, each class identified saints from that country from whom lessons on holy living could be learned. Since food and living are so intertwined, this class has truly served a wonderful purpose. It was a beautiful way to inspire the attendees to cherish their Catholic Faith and the saints and to relate that Faith and those saints to daily living through prayer and eating well. This cookbook continues that effort and provides a means of spreading the good word about the many gifts and blessings God bestows on us, at times in unexpected ways. We are grateful for those who have organized these classes over the years and have put together this special cookbook. Now you, too, can share in the fruit (pun intended) of these efforts.

— **Father Dennis W. Kleinmann**

Pastor, St. Veronica Catholic Church, Chantilly, Virginia

When Our Lord speaks of the Heavenly Kingdom, He often uses the image of a banquet—not only in parables such as those of the ten bridesmaids (Matt. 25:1-13) and the great dinner (Luke 14:15-24) but also in several direct references. Jesus tells the apostles:

> As my Father appointed a kingdom for me, so do I appoint for you that you may eat and drink at my table in my kingdom, and sit on thrones judging the twelve tribes of Israel. (Luke 22:29-30)

He also tells those following Him:

> I tell you, many will come from east and west and sit at table with Abraham, Isaac, and Jacob in the kingdom of heaven. (Matt. 8:11)

Clearly, the convivial gathering of believers is a component of our Catholic Faith — not only temporally, in the here and now, but as part of our eternal reward in heaven.

We see ourselves as mystically united to our brethren in the Body of Christ. We pray to the saints, asking their intercession; and they gladly intercede on our behalf. All the while, we share a profoundly more intimate communion through our earthly liturgy of the Mass, which participates in the heavenly liturgy. This communion is most fully expressed in the receiving of the Eucharist. This communal meal that takes place at every Mass celebrated anywhere in the world, in all time, has always been seen as the "Marriage Supper of the Lamb." How appropriate, then, to remember those sharing in the Heavenly Banquet, the saints, while partaking of an earthly repast.

—Fr. Charles Smith
St. Raymond of Peñafort Church, Springfield, Virginia

Image Credits

Image of St. Agnes, public domain, xiv

Image of St. Catherine of Alexandria, public domain, xiv

Image of St. Clare, public domain, xiv

Image of St. Francis of Assisi, public domain, xv

Image of St. Helena, public domain, xv

Image of French Dominican nun, public domain, xv

Image of St. Margaret of Scotland, public domain, xv

Image of St. Mary Magdalene, public domain, xvi

Image of St. Nicholas, public domain, xvi

Image of St. Stanislaus of Kraków, public domain, xvi

Image of St. Terence, public domain, xvi

Communion of Saints, Fra Angelico, public domain, 5

The Baptism of Christ, Antoine Coypel, public domain, 6

Image of St. Basil the Great, public domain, 10

Image of St. John Henry Newman, public domain, 12

Philly Cheesecake, Melissa Lew, 12

Cream cheese, MaraZe/Shutterstock (722175850), 13

Middle Eastern Menu, Melissa Lew, 14-15

Image of St. Anthony the Abbot, public domain, 16

Ground sumac, Nedim Bajramovic/Shutterstock (1205968618), 19

Phyllo pastry, casanisa/Shutterstock (1198046158), 22

Image of St. Francis de Sales, public domain, 24

Duck breast, bonchan/Shutterstock (504202102), 25

Image of St. Thomas Aquinas, public domain, 26

St. Brigid's Oatcakes, Melissa Lew, 29, 30

Image of St. Brigid of Kildare, public domain, 31

Our Lady of Copacabana with Saint Joseph and Saint Peter, photo by Blair Clark, courtesy of Palace of the Governors Photo Archives (NMHM/DCA), #2005.027.029, 32

Fried eggs, Lita Akhmetova/Shutterstock (647190049), 35

Red potatoes, margouillat/Shutterstock (228320110), 35

Japanese Meal, Melissa Lew, 36-37

Image of St. Paul Miki, © Tracy L. Christianson, 38

Image of St. Claude de la Columbière, public domain, 44

Normandy Apple Tart, Melissa Lew, 44

Peeling apple, Eduardo Lopez/Shutterstock (506784352), 47

Hand with rolling pin and flour, vita pakhai/Shutterstock (133176752), 47

Caldo Verde, Natalia Mylova/Shutterstock (109751024), 48

Statues of Sts. Jacinta and Francisco Marto, Sanctuary of Fatima, Portugal, Cynthia Liang/Shutterstock (646461613), 48

Image of St. Katharine Drexel, public domain, 52

Philadelphia Cheesesteak Sandwich, Melissa Lew, 52

Image of St. John Ogilvie, public domain, 54

Image of St. Patrick, public domain, 56

Cottage pie, Maria Kovaleva/Shutterstock (1102247549), 56

Cheddar cheese, Stephanie Frey/Shutterstock (1167202294), 59

Dark beer, Brandon Bourdages/Shutterstock (243338443), 59

Scallions, Zanna Pesnina/Shutterstock (1013094157), 59

Potatoes, Artem Shadrin/Shutterstock (357941285), 59

Hearty Italian Meal, Melissa Lew, 60-61

St. Joseph with the Infant Jesus, Guido Reni, public domain, 62

Pancetta, Dario Lo Presti/Shutterstock (432309127), 66

Flight into Egypt, public domain, 71

St. John the Hermit, by Emmanuel Zanes, 17th-century icon, AGE Fotostock (DAE-92000807), 72

Image of St. John of Egypt, public domain, 72

Image of St. Mary of Egypt, public domain, 76

Image of St. Vincent Ferrer, public domain, 78

Pork Adobo, Melissa Lew, 78

Image of St. Apollonius, public domain, 80

Image of St. Anselm of Canterbury, public domain, 82

Vegetarian Lebanese Lunch, Melissa Lew, 84

Image of St. Mark the Evangelist, public domain, 86

Cheddar scones, AS Food Studio/Shutterstock (392538796), 82

Saint Catherine of Siena, by Giambattisto Tiepolo, jorisvo/Shutterstock (94284007), 92

Stuffed grape leaves, Anna Shepulova/Shutterstock (1098819824), 95

Image of St. Philip the Apostle, public domain, 96

Image of St. Damien of Molokai, public domain, 98

Carbonnade, Melissa Lew, 98

Beef cheeks, DronG/Shutterstock (326069549), 99

Speculoos cookies, Oliver Hoffmann/Shutterstock (218870935), 99

Belgian endive, Brent Hofacker/Shutterstock (565724143), 101

Gruyère cheese, Robyn Mackenzie/Shutterstock (234104902), 101

Farm Dinner, Melissa Lew, 102-3

Image of St. Isidore the Farmer, public domain, 104

Index

Sophia Institute

Sophia Institute is a nonprofit institution that seeks to nurture the spiritual, moral, and cultural life of souls and to spread the Gospel of Christ in conformity with the authentic teachings of the Roman Catholic Church.

Sophia Institute Press fulfills this mission by offering translations, reprints, and new publications that afford readers a rich source of the enduring wisdom of mankind.

Sophia Institute also operates two popular online Catholic resources: CrisisMagazine.com and CatholicExchange.com.

Crisis Magazine provides insightful cultural analysis that arms readers with the arguments necessary for navigating the ideological and theological minefields of the day. *Catholic Exchange* provides world news from a Catholic perspective as well as daily devotionals and articles that will help you to grow in holiness and live a life consistent with the teachings of the Church.

In 2013, Sophia Institute launched Sophia Institute for Teachers to renew and rebuild Catholic culture through service to Catholic education. With the goal of nurturing the spiritual, moral, and cultural life of souls, and an abiding respect for the role and work of teachers, we strive to provide materials and programs that are at once enlightening to the mind and ennobling to the heart; faithful and complete, as well as useful and practical.

Sophia Institute gratefully recognizes the Solidarity Association for preserving and encouraging the growth of our apostolate over the course of many years. Without their generous and timely support, this book would not be in your hands.

www.SophiaInstitute.com
www.CatholicExchange.com
www.CrisisMagazine.com
www.SophiaInstituteforTeachers.org

Sophia Institute Press® is a registered trademark of Sophia Institute.
Sophia Institute is a tax-exempt institution as defined by the
Internal Revenue Code, Section 501(c)(3). Tax I.D. 22-2548708.